Praise for *Staying Sober*

Stories shape us every bit as much as we shape stories. This is as true for addicts as it is for anybody. This book takes us through great stories that tell the truth about a life lived in addiction—stories that cannot be denied, even by those living in denial. Ken Craycraft's book is satisfying the way great literature and philosophy are satisfying. And it has the same power to change minds and lives. Highly recommended.

—Dion DiMucci, Rock and Roll Hall of Fame Inductee

Ken Craycraft has written an unsparingly self-critical series of reflections that are ultimately consoling because they are ruthlessly honest and convicting. This book seeks not to excuse but to understand, and readers—those who struggle with addiction and those who love someone who does—will be surprised by the deep delight it brings.

—Christopher R. Altieri, Managing Editor, Crux Now

A "must read" for anyone affected by alcoholism, self, family, friends. By telling his story in union with characters from outstanding twentieth century novels, Craycraft's unique and sparkling book, with its emphasis on interior dispositions, opens our eyes to the profound and spiritually stimulating world of recovery.

—James K. Hanna, author of *The Remarkable Life of Bishop Bonaventure Broderick*

There is nothing new under the sun. When caught in the grips of addiction—or on the daily road of recovery—this can be hard to see. Our in-progress stories can feel so disappointing, so broken, so unnecessary. But we are not alone. Not only do we have a God who offers us merciful healing—and provides people, places, and things for renewal and revival—we have a cultural treasury of stories. *Staying Sober One Story at a Time* doesn't hit you with latest skills for sobriety. Instead, it welcomes you into the richness of our culture. Kenneth Craycraft offers a refreshing alternative to a society with liquor stores at all-too-many turns. There's no serenity without beauty. You don't have to be an alcoholic to be blessed by this book. The only requirement for reading it is to want to be more fully human. *Staying Sober One Story at a Time* delivers.

—Kathryn Jean Lopez, Religion Editor, National Review magazine; Senior Fellow, National Review Institute; Author, *A Year with the Mystics: Visionary Wisdom for Daily Living*

STAYING SOBER

One Story at a Time

Seeking Sobriety
Through the Lens
of Literature

STAYING SOBER

One Story at a Time

Seeking Sobriety
Through the Lens
of Literature

Kenneth Craycraft

Scepter

Published by Scepter Publishers, Inc.
info@scepterpublishers.org
www.scepterpublishers.org
800-322-8773
New York

Cover Design: Marc Whitaker, MTW Design
Text Design and Pagination: Kristin Goble, PerfecType

Paperback ISBN: 978-0-93393-238-8
Ebook ISBN: 978-0-93393-245-6
Library of Congress Control Number: 2025947496

Printed in the United States of America

For T. B., who held my hand as I took the first step.

"And do not get drunk with wine, for that is debauchery; but be filled with the Spirit."

—St. Paul the Apostle, Ephesians 5:18.

"There's no bargaining with alcohol and drugs once you have to have them. You either stop drinking and using or you die."

—Martha Woodruff

"She finally realized that when she enjoyed her drinking, she couldn't control it, and when she controlled it, she couldn't enjoy it."

—Karen R., *The Big Book*

Contents

Introduction

IN THE VERY EARLY morning of December 16, 2002, I made an impulsive gesture that could have been a scene from a melodramatic B movie. I gathered all the bottles of bourbon, Scotch, gin, and vodka in my house (there were many), and dumped their contents down the drain. As I write this sentence on the Feast of St. Martin of Tours, patron of recovering alcoholics, I can say that was the first of the 8,366 consecutive days that I have chosen not to take a drink of alcohol. It was the day *after* I had finally come to realize that alcohol was going to kill me, and very likely someone else along with me.

For "normal" people, 8,366 consecutive days is twenty-two years, 10 months, and 35 days. But I'm not a "normal" person. I am an alcoholic. At least for the purpose of staying sober, we recovering addicts know better than to count time in any units longer than a day. Today I choose not to drink. Tomorrow I will worry about tomorrow. And so forth. For the same reason, we alcoholics ought to never refer to our sobriety in the future perfect tense. Future perfect is the tense that anticipates some completed reality at a fixed time in the future. For example, when you read these words, my new book "will have been published." I cannot say that on December 16, 2026, "I will have been sober for 8,766 consecutive days, or twenty-four years." That would be to presume that I am cured of my alcoholism. I am not. I never will be. So rather than thinking about this or that milestone or anniversary, I'll just keep deciding not to drink this day. Jesus himself anticipated how addicts keep time. In Matthew 6:34, Jesus says, "Therefore do not be anxious about tomorrow, for tomorrow will be anxious for itself. Let the day's own trouble be sufficient for the day."

I have no grand philosophies about drinking—or rather not drinking. I do not believe that drinking is immoral. Indeed, I believe that the proper use of alcohol can be ordered to Christian virtues, not the least of which are the practices of hospitality and friendship. Many members of my family moderately and temperately consume alcohol, some as a daily routine. I have never counseled them to abstain. Nor do I have any weighty insights or game-changing strategies to share with people who struggle with alcohol addiction.

What I can provide—what I am—is a witness to those who struggle with addiction: Evidence that it can be treated—not cured, but treated. My treatment is necessarily related to my faith in Christ, and the suffering to which he subjected himself, and in which I am called to participate. I don't know how I would have gotten sober without this faith. On the other hand, I was drunk for many years as a feckless practitioner of the same faith. My sobriety requires an intentionality that I was unwilling to practice for the many years that I knew (but denied) I was a practicing addict.

Since I have been open about my addiction, I have had many opportunities either to steer people toward others who can help them or to try to help them myself. I have not accomplished this through profound wisdom or sage advice but rather just by muddling along. I am a man with more than enough residual faults, but who discovered that a person can get through a day without alcohol. Those who don't think they can are the ones who must.

Claimed by Stories

This, I think, is why I was asked to write this book. It is not a theoretical work. Rather, it is a book about stories and the ways they may shape our lives. More specifically, this book is about the various claims that stories make upon our lives, as well as our attempts to understand our lives by telling stories. As I explain in chapter 1, our lives are structured by stories in two interrelated respects. First, stories shape our perceptions in ways that we are not even aware of. We are "claimed" by stories, and, often, multiple stories make competing claims on us at the same time. Their claims move us to embrace this virtue and reject that vice. Second, because our lives are narratively constituted, we have an innate impulse to impose stories on them. This is so that we can try to make sense of our lives in a coherent and comprehensive way. We are formed by stories. And we form stories to make sense of our lives.

I am not interested in the debate about whether my inability to drink moderately is a function of a lack of will, a physiological disease, or involuntary happenings in the synapses of the brain. I know from painful experience that I cannot control the amount of alcohol that I drink. So today, I choose to drink none. The words and phrases that bounce around an Alcoholics Anonymous (AA) meeting (e.g., "One is too many, a hundred is not enough") are the words that keep me from drinking. And, thus, they are the words and phrases that keep me alive. "There's no bargaining with alcohol . . . once you have to have [it]," Martha Woodruff wrote in *The New York Times Magazine*. "You either stop drinking . . . or you die."[1]

But as the story of every addict is unique, so is the story of every addict's recovery. Mine has been rooted in the moral and spiritual traditions of my Catholic faith rather than the vague "Higher Power" of A.A. I seek the intercession of St. Martin of Tours. I am also moved by St. Monica, who overcame her addiction to alcohol to become one of the great saints of the Church, as reported by St. Augustine. After being told by a rival that she was "a drunkard," St. Monica, "pierced by this rebuke, . . . looked upon her own uncleanness and immediately condemned it and cast it off."[2] St. Augustine notes, "Just as the praises of friends lead us astray, so too the rebukes of our enemies often set us back on the right path."[3]

Additionally—and more to the point of this book—I have found salient resources in literature. We are, to paraphrase Aristotle, "narrative animals." We tell stories to try to account for our moral, spiritual, and political lives, for example. These stories may be expressions of our experiences. Or they may be attempts to impose a sense of order or continuity to experiences that we have difficulty comprehending, to interpret our lives in a coherent way. In both cases, we use stories to make our lives intelligible. The paradigmatic example of this twofold use of narrative is St. Augustine's magisterial *Confessions*. *Confessions* is perhaps the first literary example of storytelling as a way to make sense of a person's history. Sometimes we find ourselves in the stories of others, even if those others are fictitious characters in novels and stories. In this book, I illustrate the narrative aspects of our lives through four stories about alcoholics and the people around them.

Caveats and Qualifications

Before introducing the four novels I discuss in this book, a few caveats are in order. First, I am neither a critic of English literature nor a literary theorist. My experience and explanation of aspects of the books I discuss below are subjective and, perhaps, idiosyncratic. I wrote this book as someone who loves literature. I find sources of truth and edification in a broad range of fiction, poetry, and songs. The purpose of good literature is, in part at least, to contribute to the quest for truth. The authors I discuss did not write merely for their amusement or the entertainment of their readers. Rather, through the creation of the characters, conflicts, plots, and resolutions of their novels, they attempt to make claims of truth about the human person and our place in society. At its most general level, this is no different from someone who writes nonfiction—a historical or a scientific treatise, for example. In both cases, the author sets out to say something he or she believes is true about the world. Whether they are writing about the causes of World War II, the nature of scientific revolutions, or the human need for community, thoughtful authors make serious truth claims. In my discussion of the novels that follow, I try to account for what I think those claims are, and how I think the claims hold up, drawing on my experience of addiction and its impact on those around me. The measure of my evaluation is not expertise in English literature or literary theory but rather my own alcoholism.

Second, this book is not a "self-help" book. I have neither the credentials nor the ability to make psychological or psychiatric judgments, nor to give professional advice about the causes or treatment of addiction. Nor do I suggest theological solutions to alcohol or drug addiction. That said, I am a Catholic Christian and a trained theologian, so every word of this book is informed by my faith, reading, and training. Moreover, I believe that every problem is a theological problem, because the root of every problem is alienation from God. If we are not properly oriented toward the highest good of love of and rest in God, it is to be expected that other aspects of our lives will also be disoriented. I wrote this book because I believe others can find explanations for their addiction both by reading this book and by reading the novels I discuss. My conclusions are based upon my experience as an alcoholic as I see myself and others in the characters and circumstances of the works I examine. The theology I offer is infused through my consideration of the works of fiction rather than presented in a systematic way—it emerges from the narratives rather than being imposed upon them.

Third, my choice of the novels I discuss in the pages that follow is somewhat arbitrary, more subject to page limitations than a judgment that these are the four best books to consider for stories about alcoholics and alcoholism. Thus they are not the only novels that I would recommend as resources for finding ourselves in the characters and plots of stories.[4] The books I have chosen to discuss in detail speak to my particular way of being a Catholic and an alcoholic, and are accessible to the general reader. It is not a judgment that they are the best novels to read on the subject.

Four Novels and Four Alcoholics

With those caveats and qualifications in mind, the bulk of this book is comprised of a discussion and analysis of four novels, three expressly about alcoholic addiction and one in which an alcoholic character plays an important supporting role in the narrative.

I have found wisdom about alcohol addiction in the 1944 novel *The Lost Weekend* by Charles R. Jackson.[5] This semi-autobiographical story is a pitch-perfect portrayal of the power that addiction can have over even well-intended people. *The Lost Weekend* illustrates the ruthless and cunning deviousness of even good people who are caught in the clutches of addiction. The alcoholic's inventiveness and ingenuity in hiding and finding another drink—and deceiving his loved ones—is well practiced.

I have been profoundly affected by Malcolm Lowry's magnificent and complex 1947 novel *Under the Volcano*,[6] which I discuss in chapter 3. It is the story of one day in the life of Geoffrey Firmin, who knew he was an addict, but who tried to negotiate with alcohol. Drawing upon Marlowe's version of the Faustus myth, *Under the Volcano* is an account of the absolute obeisance that alcohol demands of its addicts and the inevitable fate of those who think they can bargain with it. For the alcoholic, gambling with drink is a winner-takes-all scam. Alcohol takes every hand. I can find myself in Geoffrey Firmin; and I can find the people who alternatively attempted to help and enable me in Firmin's brother and former wife.

The main characters in both *Under the Volcano* and *The Lost Weekend* know that they are addicts, and at least one of them makes some halting steps to address his addiction. But the stories illustrate the grip that addiction, like other vices, can have on people, as well as the feelings of helplessness of those who love them—the latter begging the question: When does empathy becoming enabling? That's a dilemma that Lowry and Jackson explore in *Under the Volcano* and *The Lost Weekend*. Their struggle to find an answer helps us to evaluate our own relationships with the alcoholics we love.

The third novel I discuss in this book is Evelyn Waugh's classic *Brideshead Revisited*.[7] Unlike the other three, in this novel the alcoholic is not the main protagonist. Nor is the novel *about* alcoholism per se, as are the other three. The alcoholism storyline is embedded in a larger narrative. My emphasis in discussing this novel is to account for the way that loved ones can drive the addict deeper into his cups while trying to help him. It's a hard lesson from a hard story. But *Brideshead* also forces us to confront the question of whether the suffering of the struggling alcoholic might be a source of grace to himself and others. The answer is not obvious, either in the story or in our own lives.

The fourth novel considered in this book is Edwin O'Connor's *The Edge of Sadness*.[8] Set in a fictional New England city that looks very much like O'Connor's native Providence, Rhode Island, *The Edge of Sadness* is the only one of the four novels I discuss in which the alcoholic character is in successful recovery. The value of *The Edge of Sadness* lies in the protagonist's first-person account of his alcoholism and the means by which he maintains his sobriety. In order to recover—because alcoholism has no cure—an alcoholic must learn *how* to be an alcoholic. The protagonist, Fr. Hugh, helps me to do that.

In *Staying Sober*, I discuss these four books in detail, entering into the narratives of the characters who themselves are shaped by the stories in which they are embedded. In each case, I examine the factors that seem to have contributed to the alcoholism of central characters, as well as the responses of the people around the alcoholics. But this is not merely an academic exercise. Rather, my purpose is to help my reader to see the real world of alcohol addiction through the fictional worlds of the characters in these novels.

Finding Your Story in Mine

The book you hold in your hands offers no grand theories about addiction and recovery. I'm not a psychiatrist or addiction counselor. I have no abstract formula for how to avoid becoming an addict or for how to try to recover. Indeed, I think abstractions are probably not adequate to the successful treatment of alcoholism. What I have is my own life story, which I find reflected in various ways in four novels that have helped me to get and remain sober. When you read this book, perhaps you will find yourself in my story or the stories I discuss and analyze. Or perhaps you will see someone you love who struggles with alcoholism or other substance addictions. And maybe by entering into the stories of these fictional characters, you might find real sources of strength to recover.

CHAPTER 1

Narrativity and Virtue

My decision to use novels as the means of describing aspects of addiction, recovery, and sobriety is not incidental. Rather, I have chosen to tell my story through other stories, because, at the deepest level, our moral lives are constructed by and within stories. This assertion contrasts with a notion that morality is an exercise in abstract theorizing. The question of what we should and should not do cannot be separated from the concrete rationale for why we should (or shouldn't) do something and how we determine which is which. This is why we cannot separate moral theorizing from the story of the Church. The concrete history of Israel, Jesus, and the Church provides the "why" and "how." No abstract theory can substitute for God's entering into the concrete particularity of human existence. We are not "abstract" beings, but rather beings whose very lives are constituted within thick, complex, concrete interwoven narratives. Any attempt to generalize moral theology (or moral theory more generally) is based upon the mistaken assumption that we can be theoretically removed from the particular demands of concrete human action. We are created in and for community with one another, and our moral lives cannot be separated from the moral lives of our neighbors. Communities are formed, defined, and sustained by stories that, in turn, form us.

From the age that we can understand our parents reading the simplest preschool picture book, we begin to form our lives by and around stories. We are all familiar with the common trope that "the moral of the story" is such and such. Looking for the moral of a story is an expression of our implicit understanding that we do not tell stories merely to be entertained or as a distraction from reality. On the contrary, looking for the moral lesson in the story is the natural impulse that flows from the reality that our lives are rooted in, and informed by, narratives. Our moral lives are story-formed. And by asking what the moral of the story is, we acknowledge that story-formed virtue is the fundamental means of understanding the structure of moral reasoning. This essential point requires some explanation before we turn to the four novels that frame the discussion in this book.

The Priority of Story over Commands

In Catholic moral theology, the fundamental questions are not "What should I do?" or "What rules should I keep?" These are not unimportant questions, and their answers are consequential. But the answer to these questions is of little value for the purpose of forming our lives as people who both desire and, more importantly, have developed the moral skill to keep the rules. Telling me that I should do thus and such, or refrain from this or that, is of little or no use if I do not have the moral knowledge to understand *why* I should, and the moral skill to understand *how* I can, conform to the mandate implicit in these statements. Put another way, knowing the rules is useless if I do not have the intellectual and moral virtues that are required to understand, embrace, and conform my life to the moral imperatives that lead to human flourishing and fulfillment.

The primary question for the moral life, then, is not "What should I do?" Rather, it is the very different—and much more demanding—question: "What kind of person should I be?" As Stanley Hauerwas puts it, "Christian ethics is concerned more with who we are than what we do."[1] To know the answer to the question "What should I do?" does not necessarily mean that I know the answer to the question "What kind of person should I be in order to do what I should?" But to know the answer to the question "What kind of person should I be?" puts me on the road both to knowing what I should do (or avoid) and developing the moral skill to do it (or abstain from it). Vicious people can keep rules. They might be motivated by fear of reprisal or hope of reward. But absent those, or other self-serving considerations, vicious people do not have the moral skill to adhere to rules because they have not learned that rules lead to authentic liberation and human flourishing.

Virtuous people, on the other hand, both desire to keep rules and have developed the moral skill to do so. Their adherence to the norms that lead to human flourishing is not caused by hope of reward or fear of reprisal. Rather, it is the product of the narratively formed virtues, rooted in a coherent story about the human person. Virtue cannot be commanded. It can only be learned. And that learning requires the development of practices and habits that are consistent with the purpose and good of what it means to be human. Put another way, the virtues are the means by which we navigate our moral lives through the snares and dangers that impede attainment of the ultimate good of rest in God and the derivative goods that contribute to that highest good. The discipline necessary for the practices that become the habits we call virtues requires the rich assembly of characters and stories that teach us how to see the world truthfully. This includes learning the skill to identify those false stories that make claims upon our lives, leading us not toward life-giving virtues but soul-destroying vices.

In his magisterial account of the crisis of modern moral theory, the late Catholic philosopher Alasdair MacIntyre puts it this way:

> If a human life is understood as a progress through harms and dangers, moral and physical, which someone may encounter and overcome in better and worse ways and with a greater or lesser measure of success, the virtues will find their place as those qualities the possession and exercise of which generally tend to success in this enterprise and the vices likewise as qualities which likewise tend to failure. Each human life will then embody a story whose shape and form will depend upon what is counted as a harm and danger and upon how success and failure, progress and its opposite, are understood and evaluated. To answer these questions will also explicitly and implicitly be to answer the question as to what the virtues and vices are.[2]

Later in this chapter I explain both what I mean by *virtue* in general and how virtue applies specifically to the human moral agent. But it is necessary to understand the narrative nature of moral convictions of any kind before we drill down into what it means to call a moral action[3] (or a person) virtuous or vicious. My purpose at the outset, as MacIntyre puts it, is to show "how belief in the virtues being of a certain kind and belief in human life exhibiting a certain narrative order are internally connected."[4]

The temptation for Christians to reduce morality to lists of commands is not surprising. We think of the very heart of the Jewish and Christian moral tradition as the Ten *Commandments*, after all. But even before Moses announced the

Ten Commandments to Israel, God began to condition his chosen people to remember the stories by which they were formed and sustained as a community. In Deuteronomy 8, for example, God's instruction to Israel is not primarily about keeping commands, but rather to remember the story of their bondage in and rescue from slavery in Egypt. "And you shall remember all the way which the LORD your God has led you these forty years in the wilderness" (Dt 8:2). They are commanded to keep the Law, to be sure, but the method of doing this is by "walking in [God's] ways and by fearing him" (Dt 8:6). "Take heed lest you forget," God commands (Dt 8:11); "You shall remember the LORD your God, . . . that he may confirm his covenant which he swore to your fathers" (Dt 8:18).

These admonitions to remember and heed are summarized in the fourth commandment, the only commandment that describes the consequence for keeping it: "Honor your father and your mother, that your days may be long in the land which the LORD your God gives you" (Ex 20:12). The consequence is the key to understanding the full implications of this command. It is not merely limited to children obeying their parents. Rather, we honor our parents by sustaining the story that we have received from them. We honor the story of our parents by telling the story to our children. The story of Abraham, Joseph and his brothers, and Moses literally created the community we know as Israel. And it is the same story, completed in the life, death, and resurrection of Christ, that preserves our days in the presence of God. Put another way, keeping the commandments results from maintaining the story. As Bishop Robert Barron has put it, "Honoring of father and mother [is] a sort of code for . . . honoring of the tradition from which one has come and by which one has been unavoidably shaped."[5]

And the story is always related to God's call of Abraham, creation of Israel, and rescue of Israel from bondage in Egypt. The point is summarized in one of the most famous passages of the Old Testament, the so-called *Shema*[6] passage in the sixth chapter of Deuteronomy:

> Hear, O Israel: The LORD our God is one LORD; and you shall love the LORD your God with all your heart, and with all your soul, and with all your might. And these words which I command you this day shall be upon your heart; *and you shall teach them diligently to your children, and shall talk of them when you sit in your house, and when you walk by the way, and when you lie down, and when you rise.*" (Dt 6:4–7; emphasis added)

Israel's very existence is created and sustained by the ongoing story of its relationship with God. Of course, keeping God's commands is never separated from the story. But it is precisely in the story that Israel can make sense of those commands. Why, for example, is Israel commanded to be hospitable and welcoming of the stranger? And how shall Israel learn to keep this admonition? By telling and retelling their own story. "You shall not pervert the justice due to the sojourner or to the fatherless, or take a widow's garment in pledge," God tells Israel; "but you shall remember that you were a slave in Egypt and the LORD your God redeemed you from there" (Dt 24:17–18; see also Dt 15:15). The very purpose of keeping the Sabbath is to remember this story. "You shall remember that you were a servant in the land of Egypt, and the LORD your God brought you out thence with a mighty hand and an outstretched arm; therefore the LORD your God commanded you to keep the sabbath day" (Dt 5:15).

Methodist theologian Stanley Hauerwas expands on the importance of narrative in the life of Israel in his book *The Peaceable Kingdom*. Hauerwas explains that the people of God, beginning with the history of God's call of Abraham, is a story-formed community. Israel did not understand the stories about its relationship with God to be ancillary to its existence. On the contrary, the story of God's call of Abraham, and, later, his rescue of Israel from Egypt, is inseparable from the very identity of God's people. Put simply, Israel is created and sustained by a story. "The Bible is fundamentally a story of a people's journey with their God," Hauerwas explains.[7] Thus, he continues, "Christian convictions take the form of a story . . . that constitutes a tradition, which in turn creates and forms a community. . . . Christian ethics . . . begin[s] by calling our attention to a narrative that tells us of God's dealing with creation."[8]

But it is not merely our account of Creation that is sustained by a story. Rather, we understand the entire history of

Israel and the Church in terms of the community-forming story of God's revelation. "Narrative is not secondary for our knowledge of God," Hauerwas explains; "there is no 'point' that can be separated from the story."[9] Put another way, we do not look for ways to abstract moral theories from the story, but rather find and sustain expressions of virtue precisely *in* the story. "The narratives through which we learn of God *are* the point."[10] Hauerwas is certainly correct to conclude that:

> the narrative mode is neither incidental nor accidental to Christian belief. There is no more fundamental way to talk of God than through a story. The fact that we come to know God through recounting of the story of Israel and the life of Jesus is decisive for our truthful understanding of the kind of God we worship as well as the world in which we exist.[11]

The Truthful Way of Seeing the World

Some readers may be suspicious about my use of narrative as the paradigm for moral theology, or even the discovery of truth more generally. The caution is understandable. In some of what we call "postmodern" philosophy and literary theory, *narrative* is a code word for the rejection of any objective truth outside of the story.[12] In this use of narrative, the story is all there is. Indeed, postmodern narrative theories often begin with a rejection of objective truth.

Narrative in their use is not for the purpose of discovering truth but an expression of the abandonment of truth. Narrative in the hands of this modern secular philosophy does not correspond to actual truth as Catholic Christians define it, namely corresponding to something real and given in the very nature of creation. Rather, narrative is a useful substitute for any kind of outdated theological or philosophical notions that objective truth exists. Truth is a "social construct" in this view. We "create" internally coherent systems of pragmatic "truth," but the story is all there is: It does not correspond to anything outside the story. It is, one might say, "narrative all the way down." *Truth* is nothing more than the word we would use to determine the internal integrity and coherence of the story. "Meaning," to the extent postmodernism even accepts such a concept, is imposed on "reality." Meaning is not discovered, but rather assigned by the storyteller or the reader. Outside the contours of the story, no truth or meaning is to be found.

Needless to say this is not how I use the concept of narrative in this book. On the contrary, as Catholic Christians we begin with the truthfulness of creation and the truths that it reveals. We receive truth; we do not impose or assign meaning as a substitute for truth. Whereas, of course, we recognize the contingency of our own existence as created beings, we affirm that moral truth (and falsehood) is no more contingent than truths of physics, mathematics, or geometry. "You will know the truth," Our Lord said, "and the truth will make you free" (Jn 8:32). This truth is universal, and not conditioned by time or place. It can't not be, in other words.

Within this context, my invocation of narrative is for the purpose of describing the quest for truth by one of various methods. Narrative in this sense does not "create" truth. Rather, stories are one of any number of ways that we make assertions of truth claims, no different in their intention than mathematic or scientific treatises. But these claims are meaningless if they cannot be tested by something outside the story. Put another way, narrative is one way of attempting to describe the truthfulness of the moral world. Narrative does not replace truth, but rather gives us tools to discover it more acutely, in all its variety and depth. Telling stories is one way of describing reality, not of creating meaning where nothing real exists. More importantly, narrative is the way that God has chosen to reveal himself to us.

We see this especially in the Old Testament, where the first and primary way that we learn about God is through the stories that Israel tells about God and itself. It begins with the stories of Creation in the first two chapters of Genesis. And we are all familiar with the numerous other stories by which God's relationship to the world are described. Cain and Abel, the Tower of Babel, the call of Abraham, the adventures of Joseph and his brothers, Israel's bondage in Egypt, the birth and absconding of the infant Moses, and the Exodus are all accounted for not by dry analytical descriptions. Rather, we learn about God through these narratives—these stories about God and, well, ourselves.

As Stanley Hauerwas puts it, "Attention to the narrative character of God's activity and our life reveals the nature of reality."[13] We discover ourselves in God's history through story. God's stories are not substitutes for truth but rather the unfolding of truth. And they equip us to see the world truthfully, to understand that God's story is everyone's story. The question is not whether the story is true or false, but rather where one stands in relation to it. The first task of story

> is to help us rightly envision the world. . . . If we somehow discover the world is not as the story suggests, then we have good grounds for not believing in, or more accurately, not worshipping the God revealed in the life, cross, and resurrection of Jesus.[14]

But to see the world truthfully *in* the story, we must be transformed *by* the story. We cannot affirm the truthfulness of God's story of Creation and redemption apart from being formed by it. The story both conveys the truth about God and equips us to see that truth. This entails learning to identify the myriad ways that false narratives attempt to make claims on our moral, religious, spiritual, and political lives. The Christian story conveys the truth about the world while simultaneously training us to distinguish between truth and falsehood. "Ethics is not primarily about rules and principles," explains Hauerwas. Rather, "it is about how the self must be transformed to see the world truthfully."[15] Thus, he concludes:

> by learning to find our lives within the story of God we learn to see the world truthfully. Christians must attempt to be nothing less than a people whose ethic shines as a beacon to others illuminating how life should be lived well.[16]

Although my framing of moral theology through narrative method might sound novel, in reality this is precisely the way that we structure our moral lives. I know of no better example of this than St. Augustine's *Confessions*. For Augustine, the truth of Christian faith was not discovered through didactic instruction or systematic exposition. Rather, he discovered the truth of Christianity through the stories of the Gospels read in community with the Church. And he accounts for that discovery through the stories of his own experience. In *Confessions*, Augustine recounts the way that narrative taught him to see the world truthfully and to see his truthful place in it. Augustine's conversion is the story of how his vision was formed to see the world as it is—to see it truthfully. That includes, of course, the ability to see and describe false pretenders. In Augustine's case, this was the Manichaeism of his youth.

We can transcribe Augustine's experience to our own, as we learn to identify similarly false claims through the reality of the truth of the gospel. We learn to see the world truthfully, and to see falsehood by its contrary. "In short," explain Stanley Hauerwas and David Burrell, CSC, "we discover our human nature more effectively through these stories, and so use them in judging the adequacy of alternative schemes for mankind."[17] The stories of God's Creation and intervention in history both convey truthfulness and train us to see the world truthfully. And, along the way, we learn to identify the false stories that contend for our lives and, indeed, our very souls. Put another way, we learn the virtues by which we both form our moral lives and recognize their opposite vices.

But what is virtue? And how, precisely, is it related to stories or narrativity?

Narrative and Virtue

Before we explore the way that virtue is acquired through narrative, we must first have a working definition of what virtue is. Only then can we find authentic expressions of virtue in stories, including fictional ones. For the narrow purposes of this book, I define *virtue* in a two-step process, corresponding to two Greek words as used in antiquity and adopted by the Christian tradition. First, we establish the *function* of the human person. Second, we must explore how that function may be fulfilled in an *excellent* way.

"Every craft and every line of inquiry, and likewise every action and decision, seems to seek some good."[18] So begins Aristotle's *Nicomachean Ethics*. As such, he goes on to explain, the good that one seeks has the nature of an "end" or "purpose." This is not merely the result of some moral action, but rather what philosophers and theologians call the "final cause" of the action. The final cause of anything is that "for which" and "toward which" a thing is directed. The final cause gives meaning, direction, and purpose to those activities ordered toward it. This final causation is also known as *teleology*, from the Greek word *telos*, meaning end, goal, or purpose. The good end that we seek is the purpose that defines proper and improper steps to achieve that good. As Aristotle notes, every action and decision seeks some apparent good—some end toward which action is directed and by which the proper means of achieving it are determined. Every action is subordinate to, and ordered by, the apparently good end posited by the moral agent. So, to use some of Aristotle's examples, "health is the end [*telos*] of medicine, a boat of boat building, victory of generalship."[19] The end sought gives direction and purpose to the means to achieve them. "Bridle making," for example, is subordinate to the good of "horsemanship."[20] Horsemanship is the final cause or *telos* of bridle making. The measure of the bridle is how relatively well it serves the purpose of riding and steering a horse.

Note that I said "apparent" good. Aristotle is not suggesting that any end that a person seeks is actually good merely in the seeking. Rather, by good in this context he simply means some goal or objective that determines the choices of moral actions consistent with the good. The "good" may very well be a bad thing, objectively speaking. *Good* in this sense merely describes what ultimate end I am seeking when I make moral choices. This leads to the next question: What is the authentic good of human action?

What good *ought* we to seek? And how should we structure our moral lives such that they are consistent with that good?

To answer these questions, Aristotle tells us that we must start by asking what the "function" (Greek: *ergon*) of the human person is. The answer to that question leads to the next: What moral actions are more or less consistent with the achievement of that function? Those actions that are consistent with the function of the person are virtues. Actions not consistent with that function are vices. Put another way, having established the function of the human person, what constitutes "excellence" (Greek: *arete*) in that function? The answer to that question will be the "power" (Latin: *virtus*) that contributes to the proper end of human moral action.

For my purposes, Aristotle's attempt to provide a substantive answer to the question of what constitutes the human function is not important. Indeed, apart from the revelation of God to Israel and the Church, such an answer is elusive. Rather, Aristotle provides a useful—indeed true—account of the general philosophical steps we must go through to determine the excellence of human action (or any other kind of excellence for that matter). This is because we can apply this general teaching about function and purpose to anything, regardless of what object or action we are describing.

For example, "we say that the function of a kind of thing—of a harpist, for instance—is the same in kind as the function of an excellent individual of the kind," explains

Aristotle. "And the same is true . . . in every case, if we add to the function the superior achievement" of that function.[21] "The function of a harpist is to play the harp, and the function of a good harpist is to play it well."[22] Thus, if "we take the human function to be a certain kind of life," he continues, "the function of the excellent man is to do this well and finely."[23] So we can conclude that, strictly as a formal matter, virtue is *excellence* of moral action that achieves the *function* of the human person. This general framework to account for the excellence of some function has been adopted by the Church, even though the substantive answer to the question of the ultimate human function is different from Aristotle's.

This framework is implicit in the definition of *virtue* in the *Catechism of the Catholic Church*. "A virtue is an habitual and firm disposition to do the good," it explains. "The virtuous person tends toward the good with all his sensory and spiritual powers; he pursues the good and chooses it in concrete actions."[24] Put another way, the virtuous person is the person whose actions are well directed toward the ultimate good of the human person. "The virtuous man is he who freely practices the good."[25] And what is that good? Quoting St. Gregory of Nyssa, the *Catechism* tells us that "the goal of a virtuous life is to become like God."[26]

This goal is derived from both the Decalogue (Ex 20:1–17) and Jesus's response to the Pharisees in Matthew 22. The Ten Commandments are divided into two tables of three and seven commands, respectively. The first table concerns the relationship of man to God; the second is directed toward our relationship to one another. Put another way, the two tables tell us to whom our lives are properly ordered, and how that order is manifest in human society. The first is related to our supernatural end of loving God. The second is related to our natural end of life in peaceable community. Thus does Jesus summarize the Ten Commandments by telling us that the greatest commandment is to love God (see Mt 22:37) and the second "is like" the first: we shall love our neighbors as ourselves (see Mt 22:39). "On these two commandments depend all the law and the prophets" (Mt 22:40).

In other words, we are created to love God and live in peaceable community with one another. To return to Aristotle's categories, these are the functions of the human person. As the function of the harpist is to produce music, so the function of the human person is to love God and live in community. The virtuous harpist is the one who plays music well. The virtuous person is the one who loves God devoutly and loves his neighbor consistently. When our lives are properly ordered toward these two ends, the entirety of our lives is orderly. (This includes, for example, our use of alcohol.) The essence of the twofold function of the human person is summarized by Jesus in the Sermon on the Mount: "Be perfect, as your heavenly Father is perfect" (Mt 5:48). "Perfect" in this citation is a translation of the Greek word, *teleios*, from which we get the notion of teleology described above in my discussion of Aristotle. The goal—or "end" or "purpose"—of Christian virtue is nothing less than becoming like God, restored to his image as he originally created us, to love him and live in community.

The means of achieving that goal is the same as the old joke about how to get to Carnegie Hall: practice, practice, practice. "The moral virtues are acquired by human effort," explains the *Catechism*. "They are the fruit and seed of morally good acts; they dispose all the powers of the human being for communion with divine love."[27] Of course, we understand that no amount of human effort can achieve our salvation. But within the context of God's gift of grace—and aided by that grace—we achieve virtue by practicing the kinds of acts that are consistent with the good of the human person, namely, to be restored to God's image.[28]

As the *Catechism*'s definition implies, the relationship between practices consistent with virtue and the attainment of virtue is reciprocal. Virtues are both the seed and the fruit of good moral action. We make choices in accord with virtue in order to acquire the virtue that more consistently enables us to make choices in accord with virtue. The practice of the virtues contributes to the achievement of the virtues that empower us to order our lives toward the good of union with God. As Dominican theologian Romanus Cessario has put it, virtue "supplies more than a description of moral goodness." Rather, "the virtues constitute real sources of human action. . . . They are true dispositions for action, operative habits that energize both the I and the *attainment* of a happy life" (emphasis added).[29] He continues to explain that the moral virtues "contain the principles required for a person to embrace specific good ends of human perfection as these are variously related to one or another of the virtues."[30] "Moral virtue renders good the doer and his or her acts," Cessario concludes.[31]

Historically, the Church has identified four "cardinal" virtues of temperance, justice, fortitude, and prudence. *Cardinal* is from the Latin word for "hinge." All particular virtues are hung upon one or a combination of these four hinge virtues. For the purpose of this book, the two most important are temperance and prudence.

Every discussion of virtue must include an account of prudence, because prudence is the "ordering" virtue. Prudence is the virtue of proper exercise of the other virtues at the right time, in the right manner, and with the right disposition. None of the other virtues are of any use if a person has not acquired the skill of properly applying them in specific circumstances. This is the role of the virtue of prudence. As Cessario explains the point:

> When prudence enables one to discover the right way to implement a particular moral virtue, then the prudent person has discovered the mean of that virtue, tailored to his or her specific condition and circumstances.[32]

This implies that the practice of virtue always involves a subjective element. Prudence does nothing in the abstract. Rather, it is the concrete application of whatever virtues are required in a particular moral action or set of moral actions. To point out the subjective nature of human action is not to say that the good is relative. On the contrary, we measure the good of the subjective action precisely by its relative correspondence to moral truth. But the concrete achievement of the good is often different for different people, or even the same person in different circumstances. For considerations of addiction and recovery, a consideration of temperance easily illustrates this point.

The *Catechism* explains that temperance is the moral virtue

> that moderates the attraction of pleasures and provides balance in the use of created goods. It ensures the will's mastery over instincts and keeps desires within the limits of what is honorable. The temperate person directs the sensitive appetites toward what is good and maintains a healthy discretion.[33]

This illustrates why temperate moral actions are particular to each individual moral subject who commits them. Temperate moral actions have an element of concrete subjectivity, because the particular actions that constitute temperance for one person may be different for another. This is because, as Josef Pieper has described it, temperance "is distinguished from the other cardinal virtues by the fact that it refers exclusively to the active man himself."[34] By the virtue of temperance, "man should look to himself and his condition, that his vision and his will should be focused on himself."[35] Temperance, Pieper explains, "is selfless self-preservation."[36] This is another way of saying that temperance is highly subjective in its applications, which are as myriad as the number of people who exercise it.

Application to the problem of alcoholism, the subject of this book, is probably the most obvious example. For non-alcoholics, the temperate amount of alcohol will vary by a number of subjective factors. These include the relative size of the person, for example, but also the times and circumstances in which it is appropriate to consume alcohol. But regardless of what contingent factors are relevant for a particular person, the amount of consumption consistent with temperance for the normal person is some amount more than zero.

Not so for the alcoholic.

For the alcoholic, the only amount of alcohol consistent with temperance—selfless self-preservation—is zero. But this requires careful consideration. As I noted in the introduction to this book, I am a disinterested agnostic as to the causes of alcoholism in general and my alcoholism in particular. In the practice of my sobriety, and for the purpose of this book, the causes of alcoholism are not important to me. This is not to say that we should not do all we can to discover the sources and causes. But for the alcoholic, that is a secondary consideration to the problem of staying sober today. Regardless of the clinical condition, the treatment will always be the same: Don't take a drink. For an alcoholic, the temperate amount of alcohol is no alcohol.

This returns us to the framework of this book. I use the four alcoholic characters in this book to illustrate that the only solution is to stop drinking. As you will see, the circumstances that contribute to the probable abuse of alcohol by the four characters are unique to each. But the solution is common. No amount of alcohol is a temperate amount for the alcoholic. As the saying goes, for the alcoholic, "one drink is too many and a hundred is not enough." This phrase is coined by Charles Jackson in the first novel to which we now turn, *The Lost Weekend*.

CHAPTER 2

The Lost Weekend

One Is Too Many and a Hundred Not Enough

WHEN I WAS DRINKING, two persistent patterns of concern recurred, one during weekdays and one on weekends. During the week, every evening brought the twofold worry of drinking enough alcohol to keep myself intoxicated for the evening, on the one hand, and of being too hungover the next morning on the other. I needed enough to get through the day, but knew that too much would make the next morning an unpleasant ordeal. By the typical blood alcohol content measure of intoxication for driving, I was drunk almost every single day for more than ten years. Part of the anxiety I felt on weekdays was that I could not imagine being able to sleep without being at least mildly drunk. (Of course, I would wake up multiple times per night due to dehydration from drinking too much, but alcoholics are not very good at conceding any point that would suggest drinking less.)

Most days, of course, I did drink too much, and the next morning was, as I knew it would be, an unpleasant ordeal. But I was what some people call a "highly functioning drunk." Throughout my drinking years, I never missed a day of work. I never missed a class, lecture, or writing deadline; never a court appearance, deposition, conference, or client meeting. But on far more days than not, I was less than 100 percent, suffering from the familiar headache and mild nausea of the daily hangover. I regretted the way I felt, and worried that it would affect my job performance. But I also knew I would drink too much again that evening, and feel the same way the next day. And so forth.

On the weekend, the worry was whether or not I had enough alcohol in the house to get me through Sunday when the liquor stores were closed and grocery stores might only sell beer, wine, and diluted spirits. I needed the hard stuff, and I needed it in large quantities. On Saturday, I had to take an inventory of the bourbon, scotch, vodka, and gin to determine whether it was enough for the rest of the weekend. If not, I had to make a Saturday afternoon run to the liquor store to stock up. I was never comfortable on Saturday if I was not confident that I had enough to last through

Sunday. And, of course, Sunday evening would begin the repeated sequence of weekday worry.

I say these were two patterns of worry. Actually, however, "worry" doesn't quite capture these feelings. The more accurate description is that these were two patterns of high anxiety. My workdays and weekends were planned around drinking alcohol. It was, to invoke a concept from chapter 1, the "final cause" of my day-to-day existence. Procuring and drinking alcohol defined my days and gave order to my actions. Nothing was more important—not prayer, not time with my children, not intimacy with my wife, not preparing for work. And both patterns were accompanied by other worries. For example, whereas my wife and family might see that I had two or three drinks in the evening, I had to hide from them that it was actually five, six, or more. On Saturday, this began early by surreptitiously pouring a shot of bourbon in my morning coffee or a shot of vodka in my orange juice to try to overcome the Friday night hangover. I subscribed to the "hair-of-the-dog" school of hangover treatment. Friday night "it had been merely drink. It was medicine now."[1]

Going out to restaurants and friends' houses for dinner or a cookout were also causes of anxiety. At restaurants, I didn't want to be conspicuous by having the three or four cocktails (before the bottle of wine and after-dinner liqueur) that I "needed" to get through the meal. For dinner parties or cookouts, I worried that my host might not have the hard liquor I craved. In either case, I would make sure to drink enough before I left home in order to achieve a baseline of intoxication. If I *knew* that my host would have only beer or wine (or, worse, no alcohol at all), I would resort either to a concealed flask of vodka poured surreptitiously in a travel mug of diet soda or sparkling water. I didn't merely need a drink. I needed to be at least slightly drunk.

The prospect of small talk was (and still is) a significant source of anxiety for me, which I go to great lengths to avoid. But if it could not be avoided, I would at least prepare for the dreaded encounter with a few stiff drinks. One of the residual results of being sober is that I rarely go to such events anymore. It is not so much that I need to avoid the presence of alcohol at parties. I've never been tempted by the presence of alcohol per se. Rather, I need to avoid the social anxiety that induced me to drink. Yes, I realize that is sometimes a burden on my wife, and perhaps even something of an embarrassment for her. I regret that. But I also know my limitations. And besides, it is less embarrassing for my wife to go to the neighborhood Christmas party alone than with a husband who became visibly drunk every time. We alcoholics know what may trigger a craving for alcohol or a felt need to have a drink (or five). For me, and many others like me, avoiding the near occasion of small talk is avoiding the near temptation to drink.

A non-alcoholic might be thinking at this point, "Why didn't you just drink less?"; or "Why didn't you just stop?" Those are understandable questions for people who do not feel like they need alcohol to negotiate the day, or for whom the occasional casual drink or two are satisfactory. It is an unintelligible question for me. I could not drink less alcohol because I could not drink less alcohol. And I could not abstain because I could not abstain. That's the best answer I could have given. Of course, the first drink was always for the initial release of dopamine-inducing euphoria. And if one makes me feel good, two must make me feel twice as good. And ten will make me feel ten times better. And so forth. But that does not really answer the question. And even as I reflect on the question as I write this book, I cannot answer it other than to say, "I just couldn't drink less" and "I couldn't imagine a day without drinking." For the alcoholic the question "Why do you drink so much?" is as unintelligible as the question to a non-alcoholic, "How can you be satisfied with one drink?"

Throughout the approximately fifteen years that I drank heavily, I had a very good life. I was (and still am) married to a loving, dedicated, and prayerful wife. Over the years, we raised healthy children, all of whom brought (and continue to bring) joy and happiness to our lives. I have had good jobs and a bright career trajectory. Yes, there were times of economic uncertainty, but never anything that caused significant distress. Although my wife and I were married very young, we have never wondered how we would pay the next bill. We never missed a credit card, auto loan, rent, or mortgage payment. Even when I left my first teaching position to go to law school (with five young children in tow), we never faced financial hardship.

Moreover, we had an active and vibrant life of faith. We were (and still are) involved in our parish and other Catholic institutions. Our children were learning the Faith with docility and graciousness. We never had any rebelliousness or significant behavioral issues with them. Any disinterested observer would describe our family as happy, healthy, well-adjusted, and, if not prosperous, economically and socially comfortable. I did not drink in an ill-conceived attempt to escape any hardship or misfortune. I was not trying to drown my sorrows. I really didn't have any sorrows to drown.[2] Of course, I would invent some from time to time. But these were nothing more than rationalizations to try to justify my drinking. I did not have an excuse to drink. And yet I drank. Too much. Every day.

But maybe not having any compelling reason to drink is a clue to why I drank too much then and cannot drink at all now. As noted in chapter 1 above, I have no grand theories about alcoholism. For the purpose of staying sober, I am an agnostic pragmatist as to the causes of my alcoholism. For some alcoholics, even the quest to determine the cause is a disguised hope to find a way to drink again. If I can determine a cause, the reasoning goes, I can just avoid that and drink moderately and happily. I am not interested in such quests, largely because I do not want to start rationalizing how I might be able to drink again. Is this a cop-out? Maybe. But I am more interested in staying sober than trying to find a strategy for drinking moderately.

This does not mean, however, that I discount plausible hypotheses for addiction. Indeed, the more we know about the clinical condition, the more tools we have to treat chronic alcoholism. This should not be for the purpose of learning to drink moderately, but rather for the purpose of not drinking at all. Having said that, if I were forced to ascribe any overarching cause of my own addiction, I would probably endorse some sort of disease model. Alcoholism runs in my father's side of the family. This suggests that it is not improbable that I have some sort of genetic predisposition to excessive use of alcohol, such that controlling how much I drink is a lost cause. Utilizing what physicians and other diagnosticians call a *differential diagnosis*,[3] the disease model is really the only plausible explanation I can come up with. In large part this is because I don't really have any other explanation for why I cannot control my consumption of alcohol. Whatever the cause, I know that I cannot control my drinking. So today, I choose not to drink. My approach is purely a pragmatic one. Whatever plausible cause(s) of my alcoholism, the treatment is unambiguous and 100 percent effective: Don't take the first drink. If that is the case, my alcoholism is similar to the protagonist in *The Lost Weekend*, to whom I now turn.

Enter Don Birnam

When Charles Jackson published *The Lost Weekend* in 1944,[4] he was a forty-one-year-old recovering alcoholic, eight years into his first stint of sobriety.[5] The novel is a thinly veiled roman à clef, in which the protagonist, Don Birnam, is very similar to Jackson.[6] Indeed, Jackson's actual book is something like the fictional one that the character, Birnam, is ostensibly trying to write himself throughout *The Lost Weekend*. Put another way, when we read *The Lost Weekend*, we are essentially reading the book that the fictional protagonist of *The Lost Weekend* tried (unsuccessfully) to write. Don could never get sober enough to write a quasi-autobiographical novel about his alcoholism. At least for a period of time Jackson did. And it resulted in his best novel.

Don Birnam is a talented but unsuccessful writer. He is also a chronic alcoholic. Thirty-three years old, he is unemployed and financially dependent on his younger brother, Wick Birnam, with whom he lives in a small apartment in midtown Manhattan.[7] Don and Wick are apparently from a well-heeled family, but appear to have fallen from the height of their prosperity into genteel poverty. One remnant of the Birnam family wealth is a country farm, where Don and Wick would spend occasional weekends, such as the one in the title of the novel.

As the novel opens on an October 1936 Thursday afternoon, Don has been sober (again) since Monday. Wick has arranged a long weekend at the farm, from Thursday evening to the following Tuesday. Wick wants to get Don out of New York to help him avoid the temptation to drink and to recover from his latest bout of heavy drinking. Before they go, however, the brothers and Don's girlfriend, Helen, are supposed to go to a matinee performance of *Tristan and Isolde* at the Metropolitan Opera. But Don does not want to go, and his argument with Wick illustrates both the cunning of the alcoholic and the frustration of those who love and want to help him.

Against Wick's protestation, Don begs off going to the opera, claiming, "Wick, I've only just recovered—it's been only three days. I couldn't *con*centrate."[8] When Wick persists, Don says, "Please try to understand. One more day and I'll be all right. . . . Tonight, when we get together in the car and drive away, fine. But not now. Wick, I'd go to pieces if I went out now."[9] When Wick asks how he'd go to pieces, Don deflects rather than answers the question. "Wick, won't you please go and forget about me? I can't see why you want me to go when you know I don't want to."

Then Wick betrays the dilemma of those who love an alcoholic but do not know how to express it, consistent with helping him to stay sober. "You know why I want you to go," Wick blurts. But then, checking himself, he says, "I just don't want you to be alone when you're feeling like this."

"I'll be all right," Don replies, "pretending not to notice the slip."[10]

Wick finally concedes, telling Don to be ready to go when he returns from the opera in the late afternoon. But before he leaves for the Met, Wick also adds that the maid will be stop by in the afternoon. "I've left a dollar on the radio in case you want her to get you anything," says Wick.

"I won't want anything," Don snaps.

Wick then asks, "What are you going to do—you're not going out are you?"

Don smiles and says, "Oh no, I'm not going out. . . . You don't believe me, do you?"

This is a conversation to which any friend, lover, or spouse of an alcoholic can relate. On the one hand, Wick does not want to treat his thirty-three-year-old brother like a child. Nor does he want to convey that he doesn't trust Don. So Wick leaves a dollar as a token of his trust that Don will be ok. On the other hand, however, from hard-won experience, Wick worries about the risk of doing so. His worry is well founded. For the next four days, Don is either drinking or in pursuit of a drink.

"Cunning, Baffling, and Powerful"

One of my purposes in using novels in this book is to encourage my readers to read the books. So I will not try to retell *The Lost Weekend* or any of the other three novels. Rather, my intention is to use the overall theme of the novels, as well as certain key scenes, to illustrate both aspects of alcoholism in general and my own personal experience in particular. In some sense, Don Birnam (as with Geoffrey Firmin, Sebastian Flyte, and Fr. Hugh Kennedy) is *every* alcoholic, sharing traits that are common to all of us, regardless of the respective variations each of us brings to the discussion. To turn Tolstoy's famous first sentence of

Anna Karenina somewhat on its head, alcoholics are *both* all alike *and* addicted each in our own way.[11] That commonality is rooted in the fundamental reality that, for the alcoholic, alcohol is "cunning, baffling, and powerful."[12] In turn, it makes the alcoholic dishonest, frustrating, and elusive. Don Birnam's long, lost weekend of drunkenness illustrates the point.

We learn later from the omnipotent narrator (who also serves both as a chorus and Don's alter ego) that Don never intended to go to the opera with Wick and Helen. Rather, he planned to spend the afternoon drinking before Wick returned for the drive to the country. It is not clear that Don was intentionally avoiding the trip to the farm, but intentional or otherwise, he does not go. Rather, he spends the weekend in Manhattan drinking and pursuing drink, much to the dismay of both Wick and Helen. When Wick returns from the opera, Don is gone, along with the twenty dollars that Wick had left for the maid. Rather than put off his holiday, Wick goes to the farm alone.

When Wick leaves, there is no alcohol in the apartment. Nor does Don have any money other than the dollar that Wick left. (Don finds the twenty dollars after he returns from his first round of Thursday drinking.) But the dollar is enough to get him started. He goes around the corner to the liquor store to buy the first pint of the weekend (keep in mind that the novel is set in 1936). But, of course, one pint is not enough. Back at the apartment, with the bottle drained, Don remembers the payment for the maid.

So, of course, he takes the money and heads back out to find a drink. That twenty dollars is more than enough to get Don drunk. In fact, some of it is enough to get him drunk enough to misplace the difference. Desperate to stay drunk all weekend, Don embarks on a spree of deceit, theft, and deception to get more money to purchase more alcohol to get more drunk. All of this eventually leads Don to the detox unit of the psychiatric wing of the hospital, where he has been taken after injuring his head in a drunken fall down the stairs of his apartment building. His brief time there constitutes the thematic heart of the novel.

"He Drank for What It Did to Him"

When I was drinking, I enjoyed the taste of alcoholic beverages. I did emphasize quantity over quality in my day-to-day consumption. For my daily drinking, the price of my liquor was the determining factor. But I also savored the "good stuff" on special occasions, drinks at the bar at academic conferences, or when we entertained guests at home. I developed a sophisticated taste for and knowledge of varieties of high-end single malt Scotch, single-barrel bourbon, aged port, and craft beer. But occasional moderate consumption of expensive high-end beverages, although enjoyable, was not why I drank. Nor was it for Don Birnam.

"It wasn't because he was thirsty that he drank, and he didn't drink because he liked the taste," the narrator explains. Rather, "he drank for what it did to him."[13] And, of course, "what it did to him" was better after two drinks rather than one, or ten rather than five. "One drink led inevitably to the next, more demanded more, . . . culminating in the desperate need" to drink. "His need to breathe was not more urgent."[14]

Like me, Don Birnam did not know why he drank. Oh, he could speculate as to some causative factors, which are rehearsed in his mind over the course of the lost weekend. When Don was a child, his father had squandered the family fortune and abandoned Don, his brother, and his mother, leaving them in financial straits and Don feeling rejected and alone. As a college freshman, he had had an ambiguous incident with an upperclassmen fraternity brother that led to a minor scandal and Don's exit from the university. But Don did not use these unhappy incidents as excuses or rationalizations for his drinking. Rather, he knew that he didn't know why he drank.

"Why did you drink?" asks the narrator of *The Lost Weekend*. Then he answers his own question:

> You were a drunk; that's all there was to it. You drank; period. And once you took a drink, once you got under way, what difference did it make Why? There were so many dozen reasons that didn't count at all; none that did. Maybe you drank because you were unhappy, or too happy; or too hot, or too cold; or you didn't like the Partisan Review, or you loved the Partisan Review. It was as groundless as that. To hell

> with the causes—absent father, fraternity shock, too much mother, too much money, or the dozen other reasons you fell back on to justify yourself.[15]

This admission, which I myself had come to even before I stopped drinking (but, of course, kept drinking), has both a positive and negative implication.

Positively, it is the honest admission that Don cannot blame his drinking on some external cause, as though that gives him a free pass. Yes, traumatic experiences can certainly lead a person to take a drink or two. But why don't most people who experience much worse trauma become alcoholics? The narrator recognizes that Don's negative childhood and teenage experiences were traumatic. Perhaps they were even causative factors. But they were not excuses. Negatively, of course, this rumination suggests that there is no escape from alcohol once a person feels like he needs it. Dismissing the excuse of external causes leaves no justification for drinking other than drinking. These factors "counted for nothing in the face of the one fact: you drank and it was killing you. Why? Because alcohol was something you couldn't handle, it had you licked. Why? Because you had reached the point where one drink was too many and a hundred not enough."[16]

Like Don Birnham, I drank because of what it did to me. But that's also why I stopped.

The most basic element of individual moral action is human agency. Agency is the relative capacity of a person to choose authentically moral actions. By moral actions, I do not mean "good actions," but rather actions that are subject to moral judgment. In this sense, a "moral action" may be good or vicious. For an action to be moral, properly speaking, the person committing the action must be free and the action must be voluntary. A moral action is the result of informed, deliberate, dispassionate choice. Any external influences that compromise the liberty, knowledge, or willingness by which an action is taken are compromises of authentic agency.

And, of course, that agency is only perfected by the presence of the virtues. The truly virtuous person, by definition, is the person who is master of his moral actions. His actions are free of force, fear, passion, and, most importantly, intoxication. As Dominican theologian Fr. Romanus Cessario has put it, "the particular perfection of the individual's moral character is always immersed in particular circumstances which cannot be . . . helpfully construed without virtue: without prudence, fortitude, justice, temperance, and all the other virtues which perfect human agency."[17] As prudence is the form of the moral virtues, so too are the sum of the virtues contained in the prudent man. "Prudence," explains Fr. Cessario, "enables a person to turn the singular reality of the particular case toward the ends of virtuous conduct, whereby the human creature most imitates the God whose wise and loving providence governs contingent singular effects."[18] Prudence is the perfection of virtue, and thus the perfection of moral agency. Drunkenness is evidence of the absence of both.

When Don fell down the stairs of his apartment in a drunken stupor and injured his head, he was transported to the alcoholic unit of the psychiatric wing of a hospital. He was attended there by a cynical, embittered nurse named Bim. Bim had seen countless drunks come and go, and he had insight into how they functioned. At the most general level "drunks were alike," Bim understood.[19] As experienced with alcoholics as he was, however, "what Bim did not see was that the alcoholic was not himself, able to choose his own path. . . . If the drunk had been himself he would not be a drunk."[20] Obviously, when one is drunk, one is not able to choose one's own path with rational deliberation. But for the alcoholic, the mere craving of the next drink compromises moral agency. As I noted earlier in this chapter, procurement of alcohol was the final cause of my daily routine. As Aristotle put it somewhere, for the non-virtuous person reason is dragged around by passion. My passion was for the next drink or ten.

Toward the end of *The Lost Weekend*, Don's girlfriend Helen finally catches up with him in his apartment after four days of desperate unanswered telephone calls and fruitless pounding on Don's apartment door. Helen does not understand why Don drinks. But she does know one thing that no one else knows: "In drink, he was not Don."[21] "She and she alone knew that he was literally not himself when drinking, knew that he was not to be held accountable for what he said and did. It was somebody else who did and said these things, not Don."[22] This was not to excuse his behavior. On the contrary, Helen knew that Don could never be himself—never someone whose judgment could be taken seriously—unless he stopped drinking. Don "needed love," Helen's reasoning goes, "Who didn't?" But "he had to get back to himself first in order to know what love was and to know he wanted it."[23]

Don himself summarizes the point in his own internal ruminations. "I'm responsible, yes, but I'm not responsible; I did it, I; but it *was* not I; it wasn't *I*."[24] Don knows that his moral agency requires his sobriety. He knows that he alone is responsible for his drunkenness. And (not "but") he understands that he sacrifices his very moral agency by drinking. By a "responsible" choice, he chooses to sacrifice his own moral agency on the altar of the bottle. Thus, the alcoholic is not excused from his drunkenness, even though it takes away his agency while he is drinking. On the contrary, he is responsible not to take the first drink.

So too was I. So on December 16, 2002, I knew I "had reached the point where one drink was too many and a hundred not enough."[25] I came to realize "there was no cure" and that it was something that would ail me always. But I "could recover and stay well." I "could recover and become an 'arrested case.'"[26] That's what I have been for these many thousands of days, one day at a time: an arrested case. It is enough.

Epilogue

I do not want to spoil the ending of *The Lost Weekend* for the reader who has not read the book. I will say this much, however, for those who might be tempted to take a shortcut by watching the Billy Wilder film. The film is very good. But its ending fundamentally changes the entire tenor of Jackson's novel. Jackson complained about this to Wilder and to Charles Brackett, the cowriter and producer. Jackson protested that "a very distinguished movie" had been rendered "make-believe" by the film's rewritten ending.[27] Later, he became even more agitated writing to Wilder and Bracket, "The final scene, as you sent it to me, . . . is an out-and-out Judas kiss."[28] The ending of the film remained essentially as Wilder and Brackett wrote it, despite Jackson's protestations.

I end my discussion of *The Lost Weekend* on this note because the ending of the novel is a far more realistic portrayal of the alcoholic in general and Don Birnham in particular. By changing the ending, the screenwriters exhibit a naïve understanding of alcoholism. The ending of the film is too neat and tidy. The end of the novel is messy and ambiguous. That's the more accurate rendering of the life of an alcoholic.

CHAPTER 3

Under the Volcano

There's No Bargaining with Alcohol

IN PREVIOUS CHAPTERS, I have said I am agnostic as to the cause and pragmatic as to the treatment of my alcoholism. My indifference about the particular cause of my alcoholism should not be construed as general indifference to the mystery and misery of addiction. I sympathize with those who strongly desire to quit alcohol but cannot find a way to do it, regardless of the cause. If behavioral or psychological therapeutic techniques can be developed through the study of alcoholism, I strongly favor research into such treatments. If neurological, chemical, or other physiological causes can be determined, so too, perhaps, may effective clinical treatments be developed. For people who cannot drink in moderation but cannot stop drinking by other means, pharmacological treatments can be lifesaving. My pragmatism goes both ways. Find what works and do it.

That said, however, my pragmatic approach would not change if I had a certain answer as to why I crave alcohol in the way that a non-addict does not. This is true for at least two reasons. First, if my struggle with alcohol can be attributed to any identifiable cause (or at least any causative trigger) outside my control, that probable cause (or trigger) cannot be changed. As I discuss below, that's because the most likely cause is related to events and conditions in my past. But second, if I could take a magic pill that would instantly cause my appetite for alcohol to be "normal," such that I could drink moderately or socially, I would not take the pill. If I have to change my brain chemistry in order to drink alcohol, that tells me that I do not need to drink alcohol. Much as I enjoyed the social part of drinking, if I need to take medication to do it, I don't need to do it.[1]

Regardless of the cause—past behavioral or ongoing chemical—a desire to drink alcohol is still a moral issue, requiring the development of the virtues by which I exercise my subjective moral agency. Temperance, specifically, is the virtue by which one partakes of bodily pleasures in a way that is ordered toward an entire life of virtue. I become a virtuous person by developing the practices consistent with the virtues. If my desire to drink is taken away by some magic pill, I cannot attribute my abstinence (or moderation) to the virtue of temperance. In turn, I am not developing the practices that contribute to my temperance in every aspect of my moral life. If I avail myself of assistance in order to practice the virtues related to moderation, the practice of moderation could not really be called an exercise in temperance. Ironically, then, the "cure" for my inordinate craving for alcohol would not come from my development of the practices that make me a temperate person. The goal of temperate practices should be the development of the virtue of temperance, not the capacity to drink alcohol.

Geoffrey Firmin's Romance with Alcohol

These considerations, among many others, are at work in in Malcolm Lowry's 1947 novel *Under the Volcano*.[2] Like *The Lost Weekend*'s author Charles Jackson, Lowry was himself a chronic alcoholic. Thus, the central protagonist of *Under the Volcano*, in this case Geoffrey Firmin, shares many characteristics with Lowry, including living in Mexico, where the novel is set. While Firmin's vocation is less similar to Lowry's than Don Birnam's is to Jackson's, the attributes of Firmin's alcoholism are a deliberate likeness of Lowry's own. When Firmin speaks about alcohol (which is often), one can readily hear the voice of Lowry. In both cases—for Lowry and for Firmin—the problem is not merely that they consume too much alcohol. Rather, at least in Lowry's telling, deeper and seemingly intractable psychological trauma contributes to Firmin's alcoholism—or at least this is what Lowry and Firmin seem to believe.

Whereas the two novels and central characters have similarities, one significant difference between Birnam and Firmin illustrates their respective authors' attitudes about the causes and possible treatment of alcoholism. Charles Jackson does not attribute any causes to Birnam's drinking. Although he does rehearse some traumatic episodes in Birnam's life, Jackson does not attribute Birnam's alcoholism to them (nor, it practically goes without saying, does Jackson's creation, Don Birnam). In Jackson's telling, Birnam drinks to excess for no apparent reason. As literary critic (and recovering alcoholic) Leslie Jamison has put it, in *The Lost Weekend*, "alcoholism isn't particularly meaningful, it just *is*."[3] Citing critic John Crowley, Jamison explains that

> the novel was revolutionary in its unrelenting simplicity and redundancy—its rejection of an abiding mythos. Don Birnam wasn't a new type of protagonist because he was a drunk. He was a new type of protagonist because his drunkenness marked him as a man with a disease rather an existential albatross around his neck. Don isn't broken by the fallen world, or the horrors of war, or the cruelties of love, like Ernest Hemingway's drunken specimens of masculinity, or William Faulkner's wasted southern patriarchs, or F. Scott Fitzgerald's prodigal patrician husbands. Don is just dependent on a particular physical substance. His drinking is pathetic and repetitive. It doesn't deliver him into the subtle clutches of metaphysical

> angst, it simply means he makes a fool of himself all over midtown Manhattan.[4]

Put another way, there's nothing romantic, exotic, charming, or mythical about Birnam's alcoholism. He is neither drinking to compensate for some shortcoming nor as inspiration to write the great American novel. Indeed, he knows that he *cannot* write the novel unless he is sober. Don's drinking is mundane, monotonous, and even boring. There is nothing redeeming in his drinking, and Jackson does not try to make Don Birnam a lovable alcoholic rogue. When Don is drunk, he is rude, obnoxious, and mean.

For my purpose in this book, this is the operative contrast of Don Birnam to Geoffrey Firmin. Firmin tries to situate his drinking in some grand theory of inspiration and mythical creativity. On the surface of his personality, at least, Firmin fancies himself wittier, wiser, and more profound when he is drinking. He doesn't drink because he "needs" to (as Don Birnam[5]), but because he fancies that his drinking is part of a grand narrative about himself. Birnam drinks to feed his disease. Firmin drinks to feed his delusions of grandeur. He believed—or at least told himself—that alcohol had a sacramental quality for him. "You will think I am mad," he says at one point, "but this is how I drink, . . . as if I were taking an eternal sacrament."[6] This is the key to understanding Lowry's variation on the chronic alcoholic: Geoffrey Firmin's drinking is part of a grand scheme of self-deception, by which his true self emerges only by the stimulus of alcohol.

Geoffrey Firmin's Alienation (and Mine)

Under the Volcano is set in a fictional city in Mexico called Quauhnahuac and modeled after the actual city of Cuernavaca, the capital of the Mexican state of Morelos. Quauhnahuac sits at the foot of two volcanic mountains, one active—Popocatépetl—and one dormant—Iztacchihuatl. For purposes of the narrative, Popocatépetl is the more symbolic of the two. It is the volcano under which sits a bar where Geoffrey Firmin spends part of the climactic scene of the novel. Like the active volcano, Firmin's actions are unpredictable and erratic, periodically erupting in a fury of violent invective and then quieting down into static remorse.

Under the Volcano opens on the Day of the Dead, November 2, 1939, with the brief reminiscence by two mutual friends of Firmin about the fate of Firmin, his ex-wife Yvonne Constable, and his half-brother Hugh Firmin, one year to the day earlier. Jacques Laruelle is an expatriate French film director (often referred to as M. Laruelle) who has a prior history with Firmin and plays a pivotal role in the novel. Arturo Díaz Vigil is a local physician and enabler of Firmin's drinking. After the opening vignette of Laruelle and Vigil's conversation, the entirety of the novel's action takes place on the Day of the Dead, 1938. Even this is somewhat misleading, however, as much of the novel is taken up by Geoffrey's and his half-brother Hugh's reflections on their respective childhoods, educations, and career paths.

Firmin's drunken hallucinations and delusional dreams also take up much of the narrative.

Geoffrey Firmin is a British ex-consul to Mexico, living in the city of Quauhnahuac. Although frequently referenced in the novel as "the Consul," he actually resigned his position after the United Kingdom cut off diplomatic ties with Mexico in the wake of the latter's nationalization of Mexico's oil reserves in 1938. Firmin's resignation is of very little consequence, since he was assigned the position as a sinecure by the British Diplomatic Service, solely to get him out of the way. Firmin "was kicked downstairs into ever remoter consulships, and finally into the sinecure in Quauhnahuac as a position where he was least likely to prove a nuisance to the Empire."[7]

Yvonne Constable is Firmin's recently divorced ex-wife. She has been separated from Geoffrey for nearly a year, but returns to Quauhnahuac in the early morning of the Day of the Dead, 1939. Yvonne has returned to Geoffrey to attempt a reconciliation, as well as to attempt to save him from his alcoholism. She, Geoffrey, and Hugh spend the day in various combinations of one another's company.

Hugh Firmin is Geoffrey's half-brother, about thirteen years Geoffrey's junior. Although he is probably not an alcoholic, Hugh's heavy drinking with Geoffrey seems to enable Geoffrey's alcoholism. Moreover, as I explain below, he has a cynical attitude toward his brother's drinking, which contributes to the problem. Hugh is a journalist, working in Mexico for a British paper, covering fascist elements in

Mexico in the context of the Spanish Civil War. He has recently returned to Quauhnahuac after a period in the United States, and is staying at Geoffrey's house. He was unaware that Yvonne was returning, and she did not know Hugh had already returned. Hugh, Geoffrey, and M. Laruelle have a complicated, intertwined history, which plays an important role both in Geoffrey's childhood and the current state of his mind on the day the action in the novel takes place.

Geoffrey was born in India, where his father worked in the British Diplomatic Service. Geoffrey's mother died when he was very young. His father remarried, and Hugh was born to his new wife when Geoffrey was some thirteen years old. Hugh's mother died when Hugh was about two and Geoffrey fifteen, and their father abandoned them shortly thereafter, disappearing in the Himalayas, never to be seen again by either of his sons.

In the aftermath of these traumatic episodes, Hugh and Geoffrey were sent to live with an eccentric English family headed by noted poet Abraham Taskerson. Jacques Laruelle, about the same age as Geoffrey, spent one summer with the Taskersons, where he got to know Geoffrey as a shy, awkward boy, who still grieved the death of his mother and the abandonment by his father. The Taskersons had six robust sons, who, along with their mother and father, were a family of very heavy drinkers, all of them regularly drinking themselves into blackouts. Thus, Geoffrey's first exposure to regular alcohol use was to its abuse. He did not observe moderate, social drinking, but only drinking for the purpose of becoming drunk.

For these and other reasons, fifteen-year-old Geoffrey Firmin could not find comfort in the Taskerson household, despite their peculiar attempts at hospitality. If anything, Geoffrey's loneliness and sense of abandonment were exacerbated by living with the Taskersons. In M. Laruelle's memory, Geoffrey "sometimes burst out crying if you mentioned in his presence the word 'father' or 'mother.'"[8] Laruelle became Geoffrey's constant companion during the summer he stayed with the Taskersons. But when the season ended, Laruelle never returned, his father deciding not to send him back. This left Geoffrey feeling even more abandoned and alienated. Mother's death, father's abandonment, and Jacques Laruelle's withdrawal all contributed to Geoffrey's dysfunctional childhood and adolescence.

By sheer coincidence, M. Laruelle and Geoffrey wind up in the same city in Mexico about twenty-five years after that summer in England. At some point while there, Laruelle had an affair with Yvonne while she was married to Geoffrey. We later find out that Yvonne had also had a brief affair with Geoffrey's brother, Hugh. Both affairs were known to Geoffrey, and are clearly related to his deeper dive into alcoholism. Ultimately, Yvonne left Geoffrey and eventually divorced him. As Lowry constructs the narrative, it is not implausible that Yvonne's affairs were partly initiated by Geoffrey's chronic drinking rather than his drinking being a result of her abandonment. Or, as is often the case, the trauma fed the alcoholism and the alcoholism magnified the trauma.

Lowry's description of Geoffrey's formative years and the adultery of his wife is not incidental, of course. Rather, his purpose is to provide some context for Firmin's later inability to control his drinking. The persistent themes of abandonment, alienation, betrayal, and loneliness cannot be separated from Geoffrey's moral, psychological, and spiritual development. This is not to say, however, that Lowry excuses Firmin's drinking, as though he had lost all human agency. Lowry does not defend Firmin's drinking, even while providing important context to help account for possible catalysts.

Geoffrey Firmin's traumatic fictional childhood has some relevant similarities to my own real one. As such, I can understand the context of Firmin's adult alcoholism with some sympathy. But a comparison of Geoffrey's childhood and mine also tells me that neither of our respective relationships to alcohol are irrevocably determined by those dysfunctional formative years.

Three months before I was born, my young father died in an automobile crash in Lakehurst, New Jersey, where he was stationed as an enlisted sailor. His death left my young pregnant mother a widow and her two-year-old daughter fatherless. And, of course, it left me "abandoned" before I was even born. In my very earliest memories, I understood that I did not have a father. But I do not remember being unhappy or distraught about being fatherless. It just was. Like a person born blind or deaf, I didn't know anything different. As a young child, I could not process being fatherless because I had nothing with which to compare it. For me, it was "normal," even though it was different from other families.

But as I grew older, I realized that the difference was significant, and my father was sorely missed. My mother struggled financially both in those early years and throughout my childhood. As a kindergartner or first grader, I remember moving from house to house because the rent had not been paid. I recall a sheriff's deputy coming to the door of one of our rented apartments with a warrant for my mother's arrest for check-kiting, which was habitual for her. A few years later, I flushed with shame at the local grocery store checkout line when I saw a bounced check from my mother tacked to a board adjacent to a list of people whose checks would not be accepted. And so I came to have a deeper sense of the loss of not having a father.

But it got worse.

When I was about six or seven years old, my mother took up with a divorced man some twenty years older than her. Shortly after they met, the man started spending the night and skipping work from his job as an automobile mechanic. Eventually he was fired from his job and moved in with us, making the financial strain even worse. My mother's meager veterans' survivor benefits were not sufficient for her, my sister, and me. Now they were being stretched even thinner by a parasitical man, whose contribution to the houschold was to sit at the kitchen table all day, chain-smoking Camel cigarettes, paid for with money meant for my family's basic needs.

But it got even worse.

Not long after moving in with us, the man began verbally and physically abusing me. He was filled with hate and rage because he was being supported by checks sent to my house in the name of my deceased father, whose name I shared. The man reveled in making up horrendous stories and vile accusations about me and telling them to whomever would listen. If I objected, the six-foot, 250-pound man beat me mercilessly. My mother did nothing to stop his violence or to comfort me. She allowed his verbal abuse, even though she knew he was an inveterate liar. And she stood by indifferently when he beat me.

So my father died before I was born and my mother effectively abandoned me, choosing this monstrous, obscene, wicked person over her own son. Every single day of my life in those days, from elementary school through high school, was filled with tension, anxiety, and fear. Mostly, though, I felt abandoned and forsaken.

Despite (or perhaps because of) this deeply unhappy home life, I excelled in school and athletics. My escape from sadness at home was to excel in the classroom and on the athletics field. I was a straight-A student and, in high school, all-Ohio cross-country runner, winning multiple accolades for both academics and athletics. But regardless of my success outside the home, I always had to come home at the end of the day, to the same psychological and physical trauma from an abusive man and indifferent, if not even complicit, mother. Eventually, of course, I left for college and never returned to my home.

But the wounds were—or rather *are*—deep and persistent. And although I was not always expressly mindful of the past trauma, in retrospect I can see that I began to drink in order to compensate for those harrowing years at home. I do believe that my drinking was at least partially caused by the futile felt need to erase those abrasive memories or at least lubricate them. But, of course, the memories were neither dispelled nor eased. And as I have noted above, I will not draw the conclusion that my sense of abandonment and alienation is the cause of my alcoholism. But it was a factor. And because alcohol is "cunning, baffling, and powerful,"[9] it taught me to excuse my excessive drinking. Put another way, alcohol fueled my practice of self-deception.

Geoffrey Firmin's Practice of Self-Deception (and Mine)

In his memoir *Hannah's Child*, theologian Stanley Hauerwas notes that we humans "are subtle creatures capable of infinite modes of self-deception."[10] Some thirty-five years earlier, Hauerwas and Fr. David Burrell asserted that "our ability to . . . live authentically depends on our capacity to avoid self-deception," something that we cannot do without "developing the skills required to articulate the shape of our individual and social engagements."[11] Our failure to develop these skills is not, Burrell and Hauerwas suggest, "a wholesale charge of hypocrisy." Rather, "self-deception remains more subtle."[12]

Self-deception is not an exercise in deliberate dishonesty, whether before ourselves or others. It certainly may be the case that we deliberately construct false histories about ourselves, and these histories may eventually lead to self-deception. But in these instances, we are not deceiving ourselves: We know we are constructing a false, or at least a distorted, reality. That said, however, the practice of obfuscation about who we are may become the kind of habit that leads us to the self-deception that I have in mind.

The self-deception that Burrell and Hauerwas describe is different from deliberate prevarication. "Self-deception must stem from a purpose strong enough that our position cannot be interpreted as a sham," they explain. That purpose often takes the form of ignoring, or attempting to ignore, indications that are contrary to our developing story of self-deception. Moreover, self-deception is not an isolated exercise of obfuscation, misdirection, or feint. Rather, our tendencies toward self-deception are rooted in larger stories by which we attempt to construct accounts of ourselves that support contradictory identities. Self-deception, like any virtue or vice, is a skill learned through the repetition of habits and practices, accompanied by some intentional purposes or posited ends. As Burrell and Hauerwas put it,

> A state of self-deception cannot issue from a single decision, . . . but reverts to a policy not to spell out certain activities in which the agent is involved. Moreover, once such a policy has been adopted, there is ever more reason to continue it, so that a *process* of self-deception has been initiated [emphasis added]. Our overall posture of sincerity demands that we make this particular policy consistent with the whole range of our engagements. In this way, a specific policy leads to a pervasive condition called self-deception. Curiously enough, it is our prevailing desire to be consistent which escalates a policy into an enveloping condition.
>
> . . . We may even feel that the commitments we have made require us to keep up an ongoing policy of avoidance. We may feel compelled to maintain our web of illusion because others have been drawn into it.[13]

Some exercises in self-deception are benign in their origins. Sometimes they are temporary mechanisms of psychological or emotional self-protection. But even these kinds of exercises in self-deception, although rooted in natural tendencies of self-preservation, may lead to unanticipated harms. As Burrell and Hauerwas put it, "Our protective deceits become destructive when they begin to serve our need to shape a world consistent with our illusions."[14] Thus, even these less obviously tendentious forms of self-deception are fraught with danger, even when they are confronted. “The very same imaginative and intellectual skills which lead us to discriminate falsity from truth also empower us to create those webs of illusion that lend plausibility to our original deceptive policy,” explain Burrell and Hauerwas.[15]

Burell and Hauerwas's account is highly resonant with both Geoffrey Firmin's attempt at self-deception and mine. Regardless of the actual pharmacology of my alcohol addiction, I found comforting rationalization in my own sad, perhaps even tragic, childhood. I do not recount these details in order to search for an explanation of my inability to control drinking. Rather, it is to account for the plausibility that my childhood trauma, like Geoffrey Firmin's, was an *actual* catalyst that became a *justifying* rationale. Put another way, I do not think that Firmin's or my childhood experiences “caused” either of our alcoholism. But it is not implausible that the sadness, even despair, of those years was a catalyst to finding false succor in the medicating comfort in alcohol. The value in this sort of self-examination is not to find a way to control my drinking, but rather in alerting me to my own penchant for rationalizing self-deception.

And, of course, I wrote this book with the hope that others may benefit from my reflection and analysis. If we can find ourselves in Geoffrey Firmin, perhaps we can avoid his fate.

Geoffrey Firmin's Failed Bargain with Alcohol

In *Under the Volcano*, we first meet Geoffrey Firmin as he drinks alone in a bar at seven o'clock in the morning on the Day of the Dead, 1938. This is where Yvonne finds him when she returns to Quauhnahuac from the United States, both to attempt a reconciliation with Geoffrey and to address his chronic alcoholism. Despite her past infidelities, it is clear that she both loves him and wishes she could help him to stop drinking. But because she seems to understand neither love nor alcohol, her efforts flounder. If nothing else, she exacerbates Geoffrey's drinking by dredging up reminders of her infidelity with Hugh and M. Laruelle.

So too does Hugh make things worse rather than better. He has procured for Geoffrey a prescription of strychnine from a quack doctor named Guzmán, which ostensibly causes an aversion to alcohol. Geoffrey does drink doses of the strychnine, but only in a mocking way. He pours it over ice and drinks it as an aperitif before returning to his Johnnie Walker. When that runs out, Geoffrey drinks alcohol-based, rum-scented hair tonic. "Not bad," says Geoffrey, immediately before vomiting into the toilet.[16] Moreover, Hugh himself drinks in excess with Geoffrey, giving the Consul rationalization and comfort. We alcoholics love company, as it helps to justify our own drinking.

As Hugh, Yvonne, and Geoffrey navigate their day—from Geoffrey's run-down house to the local Day of the

Dead carnival to a bullthrowing[17] event in a nearby city—Geoffrey's excessive drinking is the thread running through the fabric of their ultimately ill-fated adventure. At one point, while Geoffrey is passed out at home, Yvonne and Hugh have a private conversation about the Consul's drinking.

> Yvonne: "What do you think about Geoffrey? . . .
> Hugh, tell me the truth. Do you think there's any . . . hope for him?"
> Hugh: "About his drinking, do you mean?"
> Yvonne: "Do you think there's anything I can do?"

Hugh answers that when he procured the strychnine, he tried to persuade Dr. Guzmán to see Geoffrey. "But he refused to waste time on him," said Hugh. Guzmán "said simply that . . . there was nothing wrong with [Geoffrey] and never had been save that he wouldn't make up his mind to stop drinking. That seems plain enough," continues Hugh, "and I dare say it's true."[18]

And then Hugh demonstrates that he is part of the problem, not the solution: "What's the good? Just sobering him up for a day or two's not going to help," he asserts. "Besides after a while one begins to feel, if a man can hold his liquor as well as that why shouldn't he drink."[19]

Needless to say this is not the advice Geoffrey needs to hear. Indeed, Hugh's attitude contributes to Geoffrey's own rationalization of his drinking. This rationalization includes Geoffrey's half-hearted attempt to moderate his alcohol intake—to bargain with alcohol. "Well, tomorrow perhaps

I'll drink beer only," he says. "There's nothing like beer to straighten you out, and a little more strychnine, and then the next day just beer—I'm sure no one will object if I drink beer." And then in full bargaining mode, he surmises, "and then perhaps when my nerves are back to normal again, I'll go off it completely." Echoing Don Birnam, he vacuously concludes, "And then, who knows, . . . I might get down to work again and finish my book."[20]

Malcolm Lowry deliberately situates Firmin's bargaining with alcohol in the context of the Faust myths. Both Goethe's and Marlow's are referenced by the narrator and in conversations the Consul has with others. Geoffrey has delusions of greatness that can only be fulfilled through the stimulus of alcohol. As noted above, he analogizes alcohol to "an eternal sacrament,"[21] delivering the grace to him to see more clearly than others see. He returns to this theme as he sits in the cantina with Yvonne, where she has found him. "What beauty can compare to that of a cantina in the early morning?" he asks. "Your volcanoes outside? Your stars? . . . Antares raging south south-east? Forgive me, no." How, "unless you drink as I do," he asks Yvonne, "can you hope to understand the beauty of an old woman from Tarasco who plays dominoes at seven o'clock in the morning?"[22] Thus, he compares the entrance of the bar to the gates of Heaven: "For not even the gates of heaven, opening wide to receive me, could fill me with such celestial complicated and hopeless joy as the iron screen that rolls up with a crash."[23]

The Consul thinks that he alone can see this beauty, but only with the stimulating catalyst of alcohol. So he makes that bargain. But too much alcohol and he cannot concentrate on writing his book (or doing anything else), or he suffers from hangover shakes. So he tries to make the bargain to drink enough to prod his creativity but not enough to inhibit his coherence. Or, as Don Birnam, he drinks to overcome the effects of his hangover. "It's really the shakes that make this kind of life unsupportable," he tells Yvonne. "But they will stop: I was only drinking enough so they would. Just the necessary, the therapeutic drink."[24] And later he tells himself in almost identical words, "That's right, just take one drink, just the necessary, the therapeutic drink; perhaps two drinks."[25] Of course, that does not work for an alcoholic; this is all rationalization. One is too many, a hundred not enough.

In an August 13, 2010, essay in *The New York Times Magazine*, author Martha Woodruff reflected on the premature death of Hank Williams, who was defeated by his dependence on alcohol and drugs. Williams died alone in the back of his car on January 1, 1953, while being driven through Oak Hill, West Virginia.

> There is no romance in such a death; and not much in the life that leads to it. . . . When you're an addict, the rest of your life is a shadow no matter how many songs you write or places you go or people you please. Or how many good times you have, for that matter. There's no bargaining with alcohol and drugs once

> you have to have them. You either stop drinking and using or you die."[26]

Like Geoffrey Firmin, I attempted to bargain with alcohol for many years. But the game is rigged. Alcohol doesn't play by the rules. Oh, it will allow you to think you've taken a hand or two, just to keep you in the game. But when the cards are folded and the chips are cashed, alcohol always wins. And the alcoholic always loses.

Like every idol, alcohol is a false god. It makes promises to those who bend the knee, but those promises are never kept. On the contrary, once one has agreed to the bargain, the terms are changed, the goal posts are moved, the ball is hidden. Even though I was a practicing Catholic throughout my years of drinking, I often preferred to look to my own idols for fulfillment and contentment. As such, of course, I was neglecting the practices that lead to the virtue of authentic religion. Rather than giving God the praise and worship he is due, I bowed to the god of the Geoffrey Firmins and Don Birnams of the world, mistaking the creature for the Creator.

But unlike both these tragic fictional figures, I discovered that it was all a charade. There's no beauty in alcohol for the person who cannot control it—no truth, no goodness. I came to learn that regardless of the outward expressions of faith, I had allowed myself to succumb to the false promises of alcoholic comfort. Can I attribute my alcoholism to an attempt to compensate for past trauma and injury? Perhaps I can. But even more surely I can now attest that alcohol is not the answer. "I am the way, and the truth, and the life," our Savior tells us. "No one comes to the Father, but by me" (Jn 14:6). This Father will neither faint nor fail; he will never abandon us, even in our weakest moment. He only asks that we assent to his persistent offer of grace. This is the lesson that Sebastian Flyte, the protagonist of our next novel, had great difficulty in understanding.

CHAPTER 4

Brideshead Revisited

It's the *Way* an Alcoholic Drinks

IN MY INTRODUCTION TO this book, I wrote, "I do not believe that drinking is immoral. Indeed, I believe that the proper use of alcohol can be ordered to Christian virtues, not the least of which are the practices of hospitality and friendship." It is time to revisit and qualify these observations, and to place them within a broader narrative.

Somewhat early in my recovery, I went on trip with a colleague from my law firm to take some depositions. At dinner in the hotel restaurant the first night, my colleague asked me if I had any objection to his ordering a cocktail before dinner. I thanked him for this thoughtfulness, and

I said that I didn't mind at all. From the first day of my sobriety, December 16, 2002, I have never been bothered by others' consumption of alcohol in my presence. On the contrary, I have been conscientious about setting friends and family at ease. I do not want my inability to drink to inhibit the legitimate use of alcohol by those around me. My incapability to consume alcohol moderately should not deprive others who are able to enjoy alcohol as it ought to be used. As I noted earlier, my aversion to many social gatherings is not related to the presence of alcohol but rather to my anxiety about making small talk with strangers, or even casual acquaintances.

My point is not merely a concession that the consumption of alcohol is morally permissible—that it is not sinful or immoral to drink. Rather, I intend a stronger assertion: Consumption of alcohol—properly intended and moderately consumed—may serve positive social, moral, and spiritual ends. Those uses may take many forms: relaxing after a tense day at work, creating a convivial atmosphere at a holiday gathering or backyard barbecue, commemorating a milestone anniversary, or celebrating some recent achievement. Wedding toasts, happy hour cocktails, whiskey samplings, brewery tours, wine tastings, or a couple of ball-game beers can be, and for many people are, good events, without qualification. Alcohol may serve to enhance the experience and foment deeper bonds of kinship or even solidarity. These are good things, and the use of alcohol to contribute to them is also good.

It may sound odd to read this assertion at this point in the book, where the previous chapters accounted for the dangers of alcohol consumption. But that is the point. One way to account for problem drinking is to see it in contrast to moderate, temperate use of alcohol. When friends and family gather to celebrate some event, or merely to enjoy one another's company, the consumption of alcohol may deepen the experience, contributing to the kinds of transparency and vulnerability that build authentic friendships. It might sound like a cliché, but alcohol may lubricate social situations in ways that make them more profoundly meaningful to their participants.

Indeed, my point is confirmed and illustrated in the New Testament, in the very first recorded miracle of Our Lord. We are all familiar with the basic outline of the scene in the second chapter of John's Gospel. Jesus and his disciples attended the wedding of a friend, and the wine had been flowing freely—so freely, in fact, that it ran out. So, after a request from his mother, Jesus told the servants to fill six very large jars with water. After the containers had been filled to the brim, the chief servant discovered that the water had become wine. And not just any wine, of course. "Every man serves the good wine first; and when men have drunk freely, then the poor wine," the headwaiter said to the unnamed bridegroom; "but you have kept the good wine until now" (Jn 2:10).

Of course, the author of the Gospel of John emphasizes the miraculous nature of this event as "the first of [Jesus's] signs" (Jn 2:11), followed by six others throughout the Gospel.[1] For my purpose, however, the value of this scene is to show that consuming alcohol is not merely permissible but also that it may serve a social good when properly intended and ordered. By turning the water to wine, Jesus affirms both the goodness of wine and its purpose when properly consumed. As a sign of hospitality, bringing out the good wine later is an affirmation of the conviviality of the celebration. It serves to enhance the merriment, and contributes to the social cohesion of the wedding party. Put simply, this tells us that social drinking is not merely described in the New Testament; it is *commended.* And not merely for hospitality. St. Paul encourages his protégé Timothy to "use a little wine for the sake of your stomach and your frequent ailments" (1 Tm 5:23).

Like all good things, consumption of alcohol is commended for the right purpose and in the right context. Its purpose is to enhance the experience of hospitality, not blur or obscure it. And certainly, the purpose of drinking is not to become drunk. St. Paul includes drunkenness as one of the "works of the flesh," along with a long list of sinful categories and behaviors (Gal 5:19–21). And to the Church at Corinth, St. Paul declares that a list of unrepented sinful behaviors, including "drunkenness," are barriers to inheriting the kingdom of God (see 1 Cor 6:9–10). Put another way, the question about the consumption of alcohol is less *that* one drinks as it is the *way* one drinks. If one cannot drink in the way that enhances and deepens hospitality or friendship, but rather as an escape from something, one probably should not drink at all. Together, the wedding at Cana and St. Paul's admonition strike a balance in New Testament teaching about alcohol that serves as a useful hermeneutic through which to read the third novel in my consideration, Evelyn Waugh's *Brideshead Revisited*.

It Is Time to Speak of Sebastian

Brideshead Revisited[2] differs in some significant ways from both *The Lost Weekend* and *Under the Volcano*. First, Evelyn Waugh was a practicing Catholic, and *Brideshead* is a distinctly Catholic novel. With Graham Greene, Waugh is one of the two most prominent English Catholic novelists in the twentieth century, having written such other Catholic masterpieces as *Helena*[3] and the *Sword of Honor*[4] trilogy. Some consider *Brideshead* to be Waugh's best novel, and it is certainly his best known. This is partly because of the excellent 1981 Granada Television limited series screen adaptation. Starring Jeremy Irons as the narrator-protagonist, Charles Ryder, and Anthony Andrews as Sebastian Flyte, the eleven-episode television series is faithful to the book and a delight to watch.[5]

A second difference between *Brideshead* and the first two novels discussed earlier is that the alcoholic character, Sebastian Flyte, is not the main protagonist of the story, and his experience with alcoholism is not the novel's chief narrative arc. Although Sebastian's drinking plays a significant part in the novel, especially as it affects his relationships with family and friends, neither Sebastian nor his drinking are the main focus of *Brideshead*. Whereas Charles Jackson and Malcolm Lowry set out to write a novel about alcoholics, Waugh wrote a novel about the Church in which an alcoholic character plays an important supporting role. Nonetheless, *Brideshead* has much to teach the reader about possible causes, aggravating factors, and the debilitating effects of alcoholism. And it teaches us something about the sympathetic soul of some kinds of alcoholics.

The subtitle of *Brideshead* is "The Sacred and Profane Memories of Captain Charles Ryder," and it is largely narrated in retrospect. Charles Ryder is the first-person narrator of the story, which begins sometime in 1944, when thirty-nine-year-old Captain Ryder and his company in the British army are bivouacked near a massive country estate in England known as Brideshead Castle. The novel is bookended by a prologue and epilogue, in which Captain Ryder accounts for the events leading to his company's arrival at Brideshead. In between, Ryder recalls the story of his involvement with the immensely wealthy Flyte family, beginning in 1923. Alexander and Theresa Flyte—also variously known as Lord and Lady Marchmain—are the parents of four children, Brideshead (often called "Bridey"), Sebastian, Julia, and Cordelia. Charles Ryder becomes acquainted with all four of the Flyte children. But for the purpose of this chapter, the story is about his very close friendship with Sebastian and about Sebastian's alcoholism.

Lady Marchmain is from an ancient Catholic family and is personally devout. Catholicism saturates life at Brideshead, where a small adjoining chapel was a frequent destination for the family Rosary, and to which a local priest would come to say Mass. "Religion predominated in the house; not only in its practices—the daily mass and Rosary, morning and evening in the chapel—but in all its intercourse."[6] Unlike Lady Marchmain, Alexander Marchmain had been a nominal Anglican who converted to Catholicism to marry Teresa Flyte. When the main narrative of the novel opens in 1923, Lord Marchmain has been separated from his wife and family since he left in 1914 to serve in World War I. After the war Lord Marchmain abandoned his family and settled in Venice, where he lives openly with his Italian mistress, Cara. Alex Flyte's flight from the family plays at least a contributing role in Sebastian's alcoholism, along with several other factors. As a devout Catholic, Lady Marchmain will not grant her husband a divorce, and so they have lived separate, married lives for nine years when Charles first meets the Flyte family.

"Those That Can't Keep It Down Are Better Without It."

When Charles first meets Sebastian at Oxford University, they are both undergraduates at different colleges. Sebastian's abuse of alcohol is the proximate cause of his introduction to Charles during their freshman year. Because they belong to, and live in, different colleges, the boys would not necessarily have met one another but for a night of drunken revelry by Sebastian and members of his own college. Charles and four student colleagues are engaged in a quiet evening of philosophical discussion in Charles's room. "It was shortly before midnight in early March," explains Charles; "I had been entertaining the college intellectuals to mulled claret; the fire was roaring, the air of my room heavy with smoke and spice, and my mind weary with metaphysics."[7] To clear the room and freshen his mind, Charles opens a window of his ground floor rooms to the quad, when he hears "the not uncommon sounds of bibulous laughter and unsteady steps."[8] Wildly drunk, Sebastian wanders over to peer into Charles's room, leans in, and vomits on the floor. A few minutes after his friends escort Sebastian away from the window, one of them returns to apologize for Sebastian.

> "The wines were too various," he said: "it was neither the quality nor the quantity that was at fault. It was the mixture. Grasp that and you have the root of the matter. To understand all is to forgive all."[9]

"It was not unusual for dinner parties to end in that way," Charles observes. "There was in fact a recognized tariff for the scout on such occasions; we were all learning, by trial and error, to carry our wine."[10] Put another way, these eighteen-year-old boys were learning how (and how not) to drink. Sebastian's mess is left until the next morning when Lunt, Charles's scout (effectively a valet, butler, and housekeeper) had the unpleasant task of cleaning it up. Thinking that the mess was made by Charles or one of his friends, Lunt complains, "A couple of jugs of mulled claret between the five of you . . . and this had to happen. Couldn't even get to the window. Those that can't keep it down are better without it."[11]

In this short scene, Waugh lays the foundation for the ongoing story of *Brideshead Revisited* as it concerns the relationship between Sebastian and Charles, as well as the problem of Sebastian's drinking. As Charles explains, they were learning how to handle alcohol, some better than others. Standing alone, Sebastian's night of revelry was not considered unusual. "No one minds a man getting tight once or twice a term," says Charles's older cousin Jasper, an upperclassman tasked with keeping an eye on Charles his freshman year. "In fact, he ought to, on certain occasions."[12] But his company with fellow students obscured the fact that Sebastian's drinking was not confined to the occasional night of overindulgence. Rather, as Jasper accurately said, Sebastian was known around the university to be perpetually and conspicuously drunk. It would take getting to know Sebastian and his family for Charles to realize the extent of Sebastian's abuse of alcohol, and to speculate as to its causes.

Feeling remorse about vomiting in his rooms, Sebastian invites Charles to his own rooms the next day for a luncheon party, the event that begins their friendship, as well as Charles's education about Sebastian's alcoholism. Later in thc term, Sebastian drives Charles to Brideshead for the first time, but the house is empty except for Sebastian's long-since-retired childhood caregiver, Nanny Hawkins, who is a permanent resident at Brideshead. Sebastian took Charles to Brideshead knowing that it was empty of his family, and insisted on rushing out before his sister Julia returned from an engagement.

Charles asks Sebastian, "Which are you ashamed of, her or me?"

To which Sebastian replies, "I'm ashamed of myself."[13] Later, Sebastian apologizes to Charles: "I'm afraid I wasn't very nice this afternoon. Brideshead often has that effect on me."[14]

"Why?" wondered Charles to himself, "but said nothing."[15]

Charles's question to himself about Sebastian's aversion to his family can be transposed to everyone's question about why Sebastian became an alcoholic. Although the novel certainly introduces some possible contributory causes, it never becomes clear why Sebastian can neither moderate his drinking nor stop when it becomes clear even to himself that he cannot. Instead, Sebastian's life slowly but ineluctably begins to unravel, leaving his alcoholism something of a mystery even to the end of the novel. But that's the point. Waugh is not interested in giving us a clear and decisive answer to the question of Sebastian's drinking, because he understands that there is no such answer. The mystery of Sebastian's hopeless descent into "dipsomania" is supposed to remain unresolved. But in the lack of resolution are many lessons, illustrated by several tragic incidents in Sebastian's drinking career.

"I See It in the Way Sebastian Drinks."

Sebastian's reticence in allowing Charles to meet his family is indicative of some factors that contributed to the former's descent into alcoholism. Abandoned by his father when he was about nine years old, toiling in the shadow of his older brother (who had completed a successful educational career at Oxford prior to Sebastian's matriculation there), and feeling pressure from a strong-willed (if not domineering) mother, Sebastian lives in an arrested childhood. For example, even at Oxford, he carries around a teddy bear that he calls Aloysius and treats like a human child.[16] We have already seen his devotion to Nanny Hawkins, the only member of the Brideshead household that Sebastian wants Charles to meet. These are all indications that Sebastian longed for a (perhaps imaginary) happy childhood, in which his father was present to dilute the dominance of Lady Marchmain. Alcohol might then be seen as an escape from impending adulthood, and as a means of preserving a mythical, happier time. My supposition is supported by Sebastian's relationship to his father and his disastrous interactions with his mother.

Despite Lord Marchmain's abandonment of the family, Sebastian is strongly devoted to his father. His teddy bear, devotion to Nanny Hawkins, and avoidance of his family are all indications that Sebastian desires to preserve his early childhood, in which his father was present and the family intact. Although it is never explicit in the novel, it seems that Sebastian feels that Lady Marchmain is the cause of Lord Marchmain's abandonment of the family. Sebastian believes, perhaps correctly, that Lady Marchmain's devout Catholicism drove Lord Marchmain away. Thus (as I discuss below) Sebastian's relationship with Lady Marchmain is strained at best and hostile at worst. And at least one character in the novel believes that Sebastian—like his father—hates Lady Marchmain.[17]

During the long vacation in the summer of 1923, Sebastian invites Charles to stay with him at Brideshead Castle, where Sebastian is holed up alone, his family having decamped for their London residence, Marchmain House. As Charles describes those weeks at Brideshead, it was nothing short of paradise for the two young men. They had the run of the house, gardens, and park to themselves. And, most importantly, they had virtually unlimited access to the wine cellar. From Charles's description of that time at Brideshead, his drinking did not seem to be any different from Sebastian's. They both drank way too much, knew they were drinking too much, and continued to do so.

"'Ought we to be drunk *every* night?' Sebastian asks one morning."

"Yes, I think so," Charles answers.

"I think so too," Sebastian agrees.[18] But as the narrative unfolds, we see that Sebastian's drinking is different from Charles's.

Toward the end of that summer vacation at Brideshead, Sebastian invites Charles to accompany him to visit Lord Marchmain and his mistress, Cara, in Venice. One afternoon, Sebastian is out with Lord Marchmain playing tennis, and Charles is sitting alone with Cara. Cara tells Charles that Lord Marchmain hates his wife, Lady Marchmain. "My friend, he is a volcano of hate," she tells Charles. "He cannot breathe the same air as she. He will not set foot in England because it is her home. . . . He will not touch a hand that has touched hers." And then she adds, "Sebastian hates her, too." To Charles's objection that she must be wrong, Cara replies, "He may not admit it to you. He may not admit it to himself; they are full of hate—hate of themselves."[19] Continuing, she asks, "How has she deserved all this hate? She has done nothing except to be loved by someone who has not grown up."[20]

In Cara's soliloquy, she is mostly talking about Lord Marchmain. But it is clear that she conflates Alex and Sebastian—father and son—in her analysis. "When people hate with all that energy, it is something in themselves they are hating," she says. "Alex is hating all the illusions of boyhood—innocence, God, hope. Poor Lady Marchmain has to bear all that."[21] Similarly, she continues, "Sebastian is in love with his own childhood. That will make him very unhappy. His teddy-bear, his nanny . . . and he is nineteen years old."[22]

And then in a pivotal sentence in the novel, Clara declares, "Sebastian drinks too much." When Charles quickly says, "We both do," Cara replies: "With you it does not matter. I have watched you together. With Sebastian it is different. He will be a drunkard if someone does not come to stop him. I have known so many. Alex was nearly a drunkard when he met me; it is in the blood. I see it in the *way* Sebastian drinks. It is not your way."[23] Subsequent events on the boys' return to England comfirm Cara's observations.

Sick at Heart, Somewhere

When Sebastian and Charles return to England, Sebastian begins a downward spiral of alienation and drunkenness that persists through the rest of the novel. Sebastian's family's awareness of his abuse of alcohol began with an arrest "for being drunk in charge of a car,"[24] after a late night of revelry with Charles and another friend from Oxford. By itself, the incident might have passed without notice. (There was no accident, and no one was injured.) But the incident put Sebastian at the mercy of his mother's largess and, so Sebastian believes, under her control. "I know mummy will make it seem she has to bear the whole brunt of the business," Sebastian complains.[25]

Through her connections at Oxford, including with an obsequious don named Mr. Samgrass and a priest named Msgr. Bell, she is able to obtain a minimum punishment from the university authorities. After a lunch with Lady Marchmain at which she explained that all was fixed, Charles says to Sebastian, "She couldn't have been more charming. What were you so worried about?"

"'I can't explain,' said Sebastian miserably."[26]

Sebastian was miserable not because of the arrest, but rather because it had put him in Lady Marchmain's debt. If Cara was correct that Sebastian hated Lady Marchmain (and I think she was), to have to depend upon her to keep him out of trouble with Oxford authorities multiplied that hatred. Rather than being grateful for her assistance, Sebastian was resentful that he owed gratitude to the person he hated. Even worse, Lady Marchmain had struck up a devil's bargain with Mr. Samgrass, whom she charged with keeping an eye on Sebastian when they returned to school. Needless to say, this multiplied Sebastian's resentment even further.

During Christmas vacation of that second year at Oxford, Charles travels to Brideshead to spend the holiday with Sebastian and his family. Mr. Samgrass had been invited, as well, ostensibly to begin research for a vanity book project about Lady Marchmain's three brothers, all of whom perished in World War I and were considered to be saints by their sister. But Samgrass was also an abiding witness to Sebastian's humiliation and resentment for being in his mother's and Samgrass's debt. "'I wish Mr. Samgrass would go,' said Sebastian; . . . 'I'm sick of being grateful to him.'"[27]

Back at Oxford, still under the watchful eye of Mr. Samgrass, Sebastian begins drinking more heavily than ever. "It was during this term that I began to realize that Sebastian was a drunkard in quite a different sense to myself," Charles observes. "I got drunk often, but through an excess of high spirits, in the love of the moment, and the wish to prolong and enhance it." In contrast, "Sebastian drank to escape," he explains. "As we together grew older and more serious, I drank less, he more."[28] Worse, Sebastian was "drinking in a nervous, surreptitious way."[29]

Disaster strikes the following Easter when all are gathered back at Brideshead. Sebastian gets so drunk in his room that he cannot come down for dinner. Covering for him, Charles says that Sebastian has a bad cold. But the ruse is discovered when the youngest child, Cordelia (about twelve or thirteen at the time), goes to Sebastian's room to comfort him. Realizing that he is drunk, she announces it to the party. And then, as one might surmise from this chain of events, Sebastian begins to resent Charles for similar reasons that he resented Samgrass and hated his mother. Charles tries to talk Sebastian into going to bed and tries to prevent him from drinking more. "Why do you take their side against me?" asks Sebastian, weeping. "I knew you would if I let you meet them. Why do you spy on me?"[30]

The next day, Sebastian sneaks away early to Charles's house in London. Charles follows later in the day, but not before a conversation with Lady Marchmain. She tells Charles that it was cruel of Sebastian to leave without saying goodbye to her. "I don't want him to be ashamed," she tells Charles; "it's being ashamed that makes it all so wrong of him."

Charles replies, "He's ashamed of being unhappy."[31]

Then Lady Marchmain compares Sebastian to his father, Lord Marchmain. "He used to be drunk in just that way," she tells Charles. "He ran away, too, you know," she continues. "Both of them unhappy, ashamed and running away. . . . I simply don't understand it."[32]

But Charles does not understand Sebastian's unhappiness either. "He was sick at heart somewhere, I did not know how, and I grieved for him, unable to help."[33]

Fleeing the Hound of Heaven?

I have only introduced the extent of Sebastian's drinking and fleeing. As the novel continues, Sebastian is "sent down" from Oxford because his drunken behavior continues into the summer term. Lady Marchmain concocts an ill-advised scheme to sober him up by sending him on a trip to the Levant with Mr. Samgrass. Unsurprisingly, Sebastian gives Samgrass the slip, and wanders off to drink. Eventually, Sebastian disappears altogether, only to turn up in Morocco, chronically drunk. The last we hear of him, Sebastian has become something of a curious dipsomaniac, frequently volunteering to help at a Moroccan monastery before slipping away again for days at a time, drinking, only to show up again filled with remorse and a desire to help the monks in some way.

The simplest, and probably correct, reading of Sebastian's alcoholism is that he had a congenital predisposition, triggered and fueled by a deep-seated resentment at his mother for, Sebastian thinks, driving away his father. The more Lady Marchmain attempted to address Sebastian's drinking, the more he drank. The alcohol was both the effect and aggravating cause of his further alienation, shame, and sadness. Alcohol, in this reading, was Sebastian's attempt to overcome resentment, loneliness, and sadness.

But at least two members of the family, Bridey and Cordelia, believe that Sebastian might be fleeing something even more relentless than his mother's charm. At one point, Bridey asks Charles if he thinks Sebastian is a drunkard. "I believe God prefers drunkards to a lot of respectable people," says Brideshead.

Charles, at the time a rigid agnostic, exclaims in response, "For God's sake, . . . why bring God into everything? . . . It seems to me that without your religion Sebastian would have the chance to be a happy and healthy man."

Bridey diffidently replies, "It's arguable."[34]

Some fifteen years later, when Sebastian has been living in Morocco and haunting the monastery, Cordelia travels to see him. It is from her report to Charles that we know about Sebastian's life there. "He'll be a great favorite to the old fathers, something of a joke to the novices. Everyone will know about his drinking; he'll disappear for two or three days every month or so. . . . And then he'll come back disheveled and shamefaced and be more devout for a day or two in the chapel. He'll probably have little hiding places about the garden where he keeps a bottle and takes a swig now and then on the sly."[35] Charles asks Cordelia if Sebastian is suffering. She says he is. "No one is ever holy without suffering. It's taken that form with him."[36]

I do not want to defend either Brideshead's or Cordelia's supposition about a possible nexus between Sebastian's alcoholism and piety. But in the broader context of the novel, of which Sebastian's adventures are a substantial sidebar, the notion that Sebastian's drinking is an attempt to flee the Hound of Heaven cannot simply be dismissed. Obviously, one would never countenance, much less encourage, drunkenness as some sort of peculiar road to God. On the other hand, however, God's grace and mercy are unrelenting. Not coercive, of course, but persistent. Nor are we able to plumb the depths of the mystery of God's mercy. As a character in Graham Greene's novel *Brighton Rock* has put it, "You can't conceive, my child, nor can I or anyone the . . . appalling . . . strangeness of the mercy of God."[37]

Needless to say, the better route for Sebastian toward holiness—if that's where he was destined—would have been the more conventional one. And we cannot callously ignore the misery that Sebastian both experienced and caused his family. We do not know Sebastian's ultimate fate, as Cordelia's report is the last we know of him in the novel. But *Brideshead Revisited* is a novel about the grace of God. I don't recommend Sebastian—or anyone else—finding God in a drunken attempt to avoid him. But neither do I condemn him for his misguided quest for happiness.

Charles suggests to Bridey that Sebastian might have had a chance for happiness but for his family's religion. Evelyn Waugh does not believe that. Nor do I. Nor does Edwin O'Connor, the author of our next novel, *The Edge of Sadness*.

CHAPTER 5

The Edge of Sadness

On Learning to Be an Alcoholic

SEVERAL YEARS AGO, AFTER I had been sober for many years, a close friend asked me if I would ever be able to drink again. She sincerely thought that I could just drink moderately, like virtually everyone else she knows. When I told her that I cannot drink at all, she added in a good-natured spirit, "You were more fun when you drank." She meant no disrespect, and I was not the least bit insulted by the quip. That's partly because she is a very close friend, and I understood what she meant. And besides, she was right. I was more fun when I was drinking.

The mild social anxiety that I have discussed elsewhere in this book was alleviated by drinking alcohol. If I had a drink (or five) prior to going to a social engagement, I was better able to cope with my reticence for small talk and reluctance to meet new people. Alcohol lubricated the social situation, smoothing out what would otherwise have been awkward or even stressful. Unfortunately, much to the embarrassment of my long-suffering wife, I often drank *too* much in those situations, shifting the stress and awkwardness from myself to her, as she had to get me to the car and drive me home. But, hey, I was fun for a while! The life of the party, waxing grandiloquent about every topic! But, of course, my exuberance was fueled by alcohol's natural pharmacological tendency to ease social anxiety.

For similar reasons, when I drank alcohol, my wife and I hosted more dinner parties and other gatherings than we have since I stopped.[1] At the peak of my drinking, I would actually encourage such occasions, because it legitimated my drinking for that day or evening. While we had guests, the top-shelf whisky, gin, and vodka flowed freely, and for a few hours I was no different from anyone else. I was "generous" in sharing my own libation because the more others drank the more easily I could justify my own drinking. I believe this is a common attribute of alcoholics. As I said in chapter 3, we alcoholics are self-taught in the art of self-deception. If for one evening everyone else was drinking freely, that was one evening that I was not drinking "too much." Or at least my drinking was not any different from others'. "See," I could rationalize, "we are all the same." Of course, this was just whistling past the graveyard, and I knew it. Alcohol is liquid self-deception. It teaches us alcoholics to be cunning, devious, and disingenuous.

But back to the question posed to me in the first sentence of this chapter. When I answered that I could not drink again, my friend asked, "Not even if you drink moderately?" This honest question is a common one from non-alcoholics. "Just drink less," they suggest, "and then it will be ok." The question and suggested answer are both good faith responses. But they are helpful in illustrating two lessons.

One Is Enough; One Is Too Many

The first lesson from the question "Why not just drink less?" is that alcoholics and non-alcoholics are different kinds of people, and it is difficult for either of them to understand the other. Their experiences with alcohol are literally incommensurate. They are not different in any kind of ontological sense, of course. They share the same humanity, having been created in the same image and likeness of God. But whatever the various causes or sources of the alcoholic's condition, his or her *experience* of alcohol and *understanding* of how to drink differs from that of the non-alcoholic. The non-alcoholic cannot understand why the alcoholic can't simply stop after one or two. The alcoholic cannot understand why the non-alcoholic *can* simply stop after one or two. They are unintelligible to one another.

At risk of being redundant, this is a point that I am very concerned to emphasize, especially for the friend or family member of an alcoholic who may be reading this book. You do not understand why your alcoholic spouse, sibling, coworker, or child chronically drinks too much because you have never had any difficulty stopping after one or two. It is frustrating for you, because you literally do not understand why everyone can't just drink moderately. You have no difficulty, so why should anyone else? This is perfectly understandable, and I do not criticize your puzzlement. You have never experienced the way that one drink causes a craving for two, and two for three, and three for ten. And, without in any way diminishing your frustration with your alcoholic loved one—nor excusing the excessive drinking—this is the crux of the issue. You do not *experience* consumption of alcohol the way an alcoholic does. It is a qualitatively different experience for you than for me and other alcoholics. Sure, you may crave a cocktail at the end of a hard day, or a cold beer after a hot workout, or a glass or two of good wine with a fine meal. But your appetite for a drink is sated with the one or two, and it never occurs to you to have more. Thus, you cannot understand why your alcoholic loved one is not satisfied with the same moderate consumption. It makes no sense to you.

This inability to understand is reciprocal. Your alcoholic loved one does not understand why you are able to have one or two, because she cannot imagine that for herself. When I was drinking, I sincerely puzzled over this question. Why were my wife, friends, and colleagues able to drink moderately, and not even consider drinking too much? Better, how is it *possible* to be satisfied with a drink or two? When I say I could not (and still cannot) understand how someone can have one drink and be satisfied, I am not making excuses. That first drink caused me to crave several, and I do not understand any other experience of drinking alcohol. Among other reasons, this is why non-alcoholics make mistakes in dealing with the alcoholic, whether through moral condemnation on one extreme or enabling on the other. It is also why recovering alcoholics are often better able to counsel other alcoholics. Drinking for me is different from drinking for you.

The second lesson to be derived from my friend's honest inquiry ("Can you ever drink again?") is that there is no cure for alcoholism. Regardless of its various cause(s) among particular persons, alcoholism is a chronic condition. The alcoholic might be able to stop for a period of time: during "dry January" or Lent, for example. But that does not indicate a cure any more than a symptom-free month for the diabetic indicates he is cured of his chronic condition. When February or Easter arrive, the dormant alcoholism is revived, and the spiral begins again. Put simply, the symptoms of alcoholism can be addressed but the condition cannot be cured. When I decided on December 16, 2002, that I would not have a drink that day, I did not stop being an alcoholic. I started to manage my condition in the only way I believe it can be managed. But the condition did not go away. I cannot be cured of my alcoholism. Instead, I must learn to treat the symptoms of my condition so that it can be controlled.

Put another way, to get and remain sober, I had to learn how to be an alcoholic. This is the lesson from the fourth novel in our consideration, Edwin O'Connor's *The Edge of Sadness*.[2]

The Edge of Sadness is different from the first three novels in one very important respect. Unlike Don Birnham, Goeffrey Firmin, and Sebastian Flyte, the protagonist of *The Edge of Sadness*, Fr. Hugh Kennedy, gets sober early in the novel and stays sober thereafter. This is not because Fr. Kennedy's alcoholism was substantially different from that of our other three protagonists. As I explain below, in fact, a significant probable causative factor is common to all four of them. And the way that Fr. Hugh drank before he got sober is very similar to the way his fictional predecessors did. So it is not his condition that distinguishes Fr. Hugh from the others. Rather, he is distinguishable by the way he addressed his alcoholism. Like the others (and every other alcoholic), Fr. Hugh was not cured of his condition. Unlike Birnam, Firmin, and Flyte, however, Fr. Hugh learned how to treat his condition. He learned how to be an alcoholic.

"It's Not That Bad. Nothing Is."

The Edge of Sadness also differs in literary form from the first three novels, insofar as it is written as a first-person reminiscence by the alcoholic himself. *The Lost Weekend* and *Under the Volcano* are told by omniscient third-party narrators. *Brideshead Revisited* is written in first person, but the narrator, Charles Ryder, is not the alcoholic. This is somewhat ironic, as Edwin O'Connor is the only author of the four who was not either a confirmed, professed alcoholic (as Charles Jackson and Malcolm Lowry) or a very heavy drinker suspected of being an alcoholic (Evelyn Waugh[3]). By all accounts, O'Connor was a moderate social drinker during his relatively short life.[4] Perhaps this is why he was able to write such a penetrating novel about a recovering alcoholic. Unlike Jackson and Lowry, for example, O'Connor felt no empathy with Fr. Hugh's excessive drinking and thus did not need to use Fr. Hugh as a proxy for his own struggle with alcohol.

With *The Last Hurrah* (1956), *The Edge of Sadness* (1961) is one of O'Connor's two highly acclaimed and commercially successful novels. Indeed, *The Edge of Sadness* won the Pulitzer Prize for Fiction in 1962. It is set in an unnamed New England city, modeled after Providence, Rhode Island, O'Connor's hometown, in the middle to late 1950s. As the novel begins, the protagonist narrator, Fr. Hugh Kennedy, is a fifty-five-year-old Catholic priest, serving as the pastor of Old St. Paul's, a declining parish in a run-down, multiethnic region of his city. Fr. Hugh tells the story of his relationship with another Irish Catholic family, the Carmodys, headed by the irascible and morally suspect Charlie Carmody. The family includes Fr. John Carmody,

Fr. Hugh's best friend since childhood. The two priests were in seminary together, and were ordained in the same cohort.

For the purpose of the book you are reading, the central narrative of *The Edge of Sadness* is less important than Fr. Hugh's backstory, which he tells in retrospect in the novel. But we get the first hint of that story in an opening vignette: a party that Charlie Carmody throws for himself to celebrate his eighty-first birthday, inviting Fr. Hugh, Charlie's adult children (including Fr. John), and Charlie's married grandson and his wife. As I will explain below, this is the first gathering of the kind that Fr. Hugh has attended since he returned from a long stay in a rehabilitation clinic. Thus, he is facing a new kind of temptation among a group of people who either do not know about Father's alcoholism or, if they do know, do not know how to understand it.

When Fr. Hugh arrives at Charlie Carmody's birthday party, the reader is not yet aware of Father's alcoholism. But two episodes give us early hints. Charlie greets Fr. Hugh by saying, "It's grand to see you. And grand to see you here in the house again. It's been a long time between drinks as the poet says."[5] As the words came out of Charlie's mouth, Fr. Hugh noted "a slight but curious change" on his face as though Charlie was "actually embarrassed."

Fr. Hugh wonders, "Did he suspect that this convivial poet's phrase had a peculiar inappropriateness when addressed to me?"[6] Fr. Hugh lets the matter drop, as Charlie is distracted by other guests. Was the change in Charlie's face real? Or was it something that Fr. Hugh imagined, still self-conscious about his condition? And if Charlie's countenance did actually change, was it really from embarrassment? Or was it from reproachment? Or puzzlement? We only have Fr. Hugh's spare report of the brief interaction, and it may be accurate. But we also must take into account Fr. Hugh's sensitivity to any discussion of alcohol, especially when it is not clear who knows what.

In the second early clue to Fr. Hugh's condition, he describes being offered a glass of wine by Charlie's maid, Agnes. "Have a glass of sherry wine, Father," entreats Agnes. "It builds up the blood."[7]

As in the earlier scene with Charlie, Fr. Hugh asks himself, "Was it my imagination, or had the room suddenly become quieter?"

When he declines, Agnes insists, "Ah, there's nothin' to this stuff, Father. . . . A little sherry wine never hurt no one. It's no more than milk, hardly. They give it to babies to settle their stomachs."[8] This is a common experience for us alcoholics when invited to a party or other event at which we are not well known, or by someone who is not aware of our chronic condition. It is an experience that we must learn to accommodate by any variety of means.

As Fr. Hugh accounts for it, there's neither a set formula nor a sure reaction. "Are there such things as Firm Phrases for the New Teetotaler? Convincing variations on the prim 'No-thank-you'?" he wonders. "Undoubtedly; but I didn't know them. I said only, 'I'll pass it up this time, Agnes.'"[9]

Agnes is not ready to take Fr. Hugh's no for an answer, until she is steered away by one of Charlie's children, Helen, Fr. Hugh's closest friend in the Carmody clan after Fr. John. Giving Helen "a look of frank and total disbelief," Agnes, "muttering" to herself "moved off, and the moment was over."[10] And yet, it was not over, at least in the ruminations of Fr. Hugh.

"I knew that just a few seconds ago a tension, a watchfulness had been there—and indeed, how could it not have been? For after all, the irresistible attraction had been on hand: The Temptation of Fr. Kennedy."[11]

Sensing the awkwardness, Helen says to Fr. Hugh, "Ah, Hugh, we're not doing very well by you, are we? I'm sorry. Is it bad?"[12]

"Not that bad," Father replies. "Nothing is."[13]

Fr. Hugh had experienced something common to us alcoholics, especially early in our sobriety, as Father was in this instance.[14] On the one hand, we have come to terms with our inability to drink and are becoming somewhat more comfortable with social situations in which alcohol is freely consumed. People around us, however, are often not aware, as with Agnes. Or those who are aware, such as Helen, are never sure how to act around us when alcohol is being consumed. It is an inherently awkward social situation through which one must just learn to muddle along. But, as Fr. Hugh says to Helen to end the scene, it's "not that bad. Nothing is." In other words, nothing is as bad as being controlled by alcohol, once a person realizes he is under its control. No number of awkward encounters, no incidents of social *faux pas*, no jocular "Come on, one's not going to hurt," no need to give a firm and final no. None of these things is nearly as bad as waking up one day and knowing that you are powerless over alcohol. Nothing is.

Trauma and Alcohol

Unless the reader already knows the basic outline of the novel, these birthday party incidents are the first clues that Fr. Hugh doesn't drink. This is not surprising. As Father says in the first sentence of the book, "This story at no point becomes my own. I am in it—good heavens, I'm in it to the point of almost never being out of it!—but the story belongs, all of it, to the Carmodys, and my own part, while substantial enough, was never really of any great significance at all."[15] Whereas even first-person narrators can be wrong (or self-deceived) about the story they are telling, in this instance, Fr. Hugh is correct. The story is mostly about the Carmody family, especially cantankerous Charlie and his strained relationship with his children. And Fr. Hugh's struggle with alcoholism after a relatively brief account of his decline and recovery is not the central narrative arc of the novel. Indeed, writing in *The New Yorker* in 1961, John Kenneth Galbraith complained that despite "advance billing" intimating otherwise, Fr. Hugh's alcoholism "forms only a small and not wholly plausible part of the story."[16] Galbraith is wrong on both counts. Although Fr. Hugh's period of drinking is a very small part of the narrative, his life as a recovering alcoholic informs every page of the novel, including the climactic final scenes. As to the accusation that O'Connor's account of Fr. Hugh's alcoholism is "not wholly plausible," this is an example of the mutual unintelligibility between the alcoholic and non-alcoholic. A non-alcoholic can never be the judge of the plausibility of an alcoholic's relationship to alcohol. O'Connor's account of Fr. Hugh's recovery from alcoholism is entirely plausible. But perhaps it is intelligible only from the perspective of a fellow alcoholic.

Having said that, it is indeed true that Fr. Hugh's struggle with excessive drinking is not the centerpiece of the novel, as it is with Don Birnam and Geoffrey Firmin in *The Lost Weekend* and *Under the Volcano*. Neither does Fr. Hugh *seem* to struggle with his condition once he has stopped drinking. But that's ok. The novel is not about Fr. Hugh's alcoholism but rather about Fr. Hugh the recovering alcoholic, who teaches us how to be an alcoholic.

Earlier in this chapter, I noted that at least one common thread ties together the four alcoholic characters in the four novels I have discussed in this book. That thread is a traumatic experience in reference to an absent father. Don Birnam's father abandoned his wife and children when Don was young. Geoffrey Firmin's mother died while he was very young, and his father disappeared when he was about fifteen years old. Sebastian Flyte's father left to fight in World War I when Sebastian was about nine years old and never returned to the family.[17] In each case, the respective authors posit a causal nexus between these traumatic experiences with their characters' fathers and their later alcoholism. None of them excuse their characters, of course. Neither do the authors contend that "but for" these events, their characters would not have become alcoholics. Nor do they eliminate other factors, such as unresolved sexuality (Don Birnham), adultery and divorce (Geoffrey Firmin), or overbearingly oppressive mothers (Sebastian Flyte), for example. But the single common thread of absent fathers—admittedly read through the lens of my own traumatic childhood—is a plausible factor in their later abuse of alcohol.

Hugh Kennedy's mother died in an influenza epidemic (presumably the Spanish Flu) when he was very young. Young Hugh's father probably never recovered from his wife's death, and he had a difficult time talking to Hugh about his deceased mother. "I had only the faintest recollections of her," Fr. Hugh later explains,

> And here my father had been of little help: on the subject of my mother he had been curiously reticent. I wondered about this often, of course, although I never questioned him. I think, now, that the truth was simply this: that her death had been without question the great catastrophe of his life, striking him so harshly and with such finality that he never really got over it and could not bring himself to talk about her as she had been, not even after all the years, not even to me.

> And while he spoke of my mother often and fondly to me, he always did so incompletely, in a strangely peripheral way, so that I grew up with a picture of her that was really little more than an outline.[18]

Fr. Hugh tries not to begrudge his father's inability to cope with the grief from his wife's death. "Was this unfair, an injustice to me?" he wonders. "It must seem so, and I suppose in a way it was. And yet we all have within ourselves those private spaces that are uniquely our own and that we cannot share. This was my father's: the heart of his grief, which he chose not to expose."[19]

The context of this recollection is the impending death of Fr. Hugh's own father some five years or so before the beginning of the narrative. Ruminations about his deceased mother are intertwined with thoughts about caring for his father after he is diagnosed with incurable gastrointestinal cancer and given no more than six months to live.[20] I will not recount the full details of Fr. Hugh's last weeks with his father, as the latter's health begins to deteriorate and the pain begins to increase. It suffices to say that Fr. Hugh loved his father dearly and hated to see him suffer. "It was an agonizing time," Fr. Hugh observes about the last days of his father's life—"although when I say this I'm speaking selfishly, because what I really mean is that it was an agonizing time for me. What it was for my father no one could tell."[21]

Eschewing the duties of his parish, Fr. Hugh spent as much time as he could with his father, watching him waste away and, as predicted, die not long after his cancer diagnosis. "All through his illness . . . I had prayed that he might be allowed either the miracle of recovery or the blessing of a happy death," Fr. Hugh remembers. "These prayers were not answered. My father did not recover, and he died witless and in pain. . . . He was a very good man who . . . died a very cruel death."[22]

As Fr. Hugh recounts this experience, at least immediately after his father died, he is more traumatized by his father's great suffering before his death than by the death itself. "This is the hardest sort of thing to accept," he observes; "for some, it's impossible."[23] He is well acquainted with typical theodicies—theological arguments reconciling pain and suffering with an omnipotent and all-loving God. But in the crucible of grief, these arguments leave him empty. "A syllogism does not support a mother who has seen her baby burned," he sadly notes.[24] "When someone stands fixed and helpless before another's suffering—especially in those cases when those who suffer are plainly innocent of any guilt—then the cool light of reason may not be of much help," he observes. Fr. Hugh's faith does not waiver, at least not expressly. "While there was ache and grief enough," he explains, "there was certainly never the slightest thought of . . . turning away from God because of an unanswered prayer."[25] Rather, "If one accepts God, one accepts him totally, accepts what he does and what he permits," he states. "One accepts it, but one does not necessarily understand it."[26]

"We Depend upon Each Other. . . . We're Meant To. In a Way, That's What It's All About."

But like his father's inability to fully come to terms with the death of Fr. Hugh's mother, so Fr. Hugh was unable to cope with the death of his father. He does not lose faith. What does happen, though, "happened much more slowly and subtly, and without my quite realizing, for a long time, that anything was happening at all," he remembers. "Shortly after my father's death my life began to change, and it was now that I began to do heavily and steadily what before I had done lightly, occasionally, and in a very different spirit, that I began to drink seriously, and to my own danger, and to the danger of my parish."[27] In the same way that the alcoholics discussed in previous chapters tried to cope with trauma (or the memory of trauma), so Fr. Hugh turns to alcohol. His is not a pretty story, he confesses, and the details are humiliating, especially because he is a priest. "For here there is a double betrayal: of the dignity of a man, of the sacredness of a vocation."[28]

As Fr. Hugh begins to drink more, he associates with other people less. He spends time alone in his room or walking randomly around the neighborhood. Eventually he begins to refer every parishioner to one of his two curates, "regularly [sending] down word that I was 'out.'"[29] The more Father drinks, the more his curates begin to feel alienated from him, and the rectory becomes filled with tension and confusion. Still not able to come to terms with the death of his father, Fr. Hugh sinks more deeply into his cups. As he summarizes his despair, he says that he would

> pour myself a small drink—which seemed to help, go back to my chair, and begin again the farce of preparing to get down to work. And in a while the whole procedure would be repeated, and then, later, it would be repeated again. The only change was one of emphasis; as time went by, the small drink got no smaller. Slowly it became more important, and over the months the occasional help came to be the steady necessity. At all hours; at night so that I might sleep; the first thing in the morning, to deaden the passage into the long, dull empty ache of the day.[30]

Having come to the realization that he is drinking too much—and that it is out of control—Fr. Hugh begins to negotiate with alcohol. "I . . . reminded myself that this had become a habit, and that habit could be broken with a strong will; I got to my feet; I made a firm resolve."[31]

"The firm resolved lasted for twenty-four hours."

It is succeeded by another resolution, "then another . . . and another," each shorter than the previous one.[32] He becomes less and less discreet about his drinking, often appearing drunk in the rectory, and once even passing out on the hallway floor, from which he is assisted to his room by his curates. This leads, of course, to a summons to the office of the bishop. The bishop is kindly and sympathetic, even putting his finger on the catalyst to Father's drinking. The bishop's asks Fr. Hugh, "How long has this been going on?"; and then posits an answer to his own question: "Since your father died?"[33] After a brief and kind exchange, in which the bishop indicated his unwillingness to humiliate Fr. Hugh, the bishop says simply, "Father: I want you to stop."[34]

And he did. For two months. But then one day, suddenly and without warning, Fr. Hugh says, "I found myself for the first time in weeks smothered by this unaccountable sadness. . . . It was a mood of despair I couldn't shake."[35] This time, all discretion fell away. "The rectory secret was now a secret no longer. . . . the pastor became the public scandal."[36] This time, as well, the bishop was more decisive. He removed Fr. Hugh from the pastorate of his parish, and shipped him to a residential alcohol rehabilitation facility in Arizona, called the Cenacle. "Independent effort is all very well" said the bishop, "but if you're really in trouble, I think it's seldom good enough. We depend on each other, Father. All of us. We're meant to. In a way, that's what it's all about."[37]

Learning to Be an Alcoholic

So Fr. Hugh was packed away to the Cenacle where, against everyone's expectations, he stayed for four years. O'Connor does not give us much information of the kinds of therapy Fr. Hugh received at the Cenacle, nor the relative extent to which he struggled under the new regime. What we do know, however, is that this is where Fr. Hugh properly learned how to be an alcoholic. Whatever treatment he received there, "it worked," he explains later. "I did what I could not have done alone: I came to terms with myself; I came to terms with God."[38]

This returns me to the purpose of the book you are reading. We alcoholics will not be cured of our alcoholism. It is a permanent, chronic condition for which there is no known remedy. Instead of looking for a cure that cannot be found, then, the goal of the recovering alcoholic is to learn the proper way to be an alcoholic.

Again, O'Connor does not tell us what skills Father learned or what kinds of therapy he experienced. But through Fr. Hugh's resumed ministry after his return, and the reinvigoration of his friendship with the Carmodys (remember them?), we see that Fr. Hugh has indeed learned both how to be an alcoholic, and also how to use those skills to be present to others. Earlier, I cited J. K. Galbraith's complaint that *The Edge of Sadness* is not really about alcoholism. It isn't. But Galbraith was accusing the novel of doing something O'Connor did not intend. The novel is not supposed to be about Fr. Hugh's alcoholism. Rather, it's about his life as a recovering alcoholic, having learned how to be an alcoholic. And having developed the skills to be a good alcoholic, Fr. Hugh gradually learned how to be a witness to others of constancy, determination, fortitude, empathy, and, of course, faith.

Without spoiling the end of the novel, Fr. Hugh is called upon by the Carmodys to bear a heavy burden—nay, several heavy burdens—as the dark secrets of the Carmodys are exposed. None of them suffer from alcoholism. But all of them suffer various other spiritual, moral, behavioral, and psychological pathologies. And it is the pastor who "became the public scandal" that is uniquely suited to bear those burdens. I wondered in the previous chapter whether any grace could be found in Sebastian Flyte's alcoholism, as his sister Cordelia believed. In *The Edge of Sadness*, Edwin O'Connor offers a way of answering the question in the affirmative. Of course, no one would wish for Fr. Hugh to become an alcoholic, nor to suffer the triggering despondency of his father's death. But as O'Connor constructs the narrative, it was *because* he learned how to be an alcoholic that he was able to minister to the wildly dysfunctional Carmodys at the end of the novel.

In telling his story, Fr. Hugh uses the phrase "the edge of sadness" twice. The first is a description of his conversation with Helen Carmody, with whom Father was very close. Again, without spoiling the novel, Helen has been affected by her father, Charlie, in ways that were not apparent until the end of the book. The difficult relationship with him led her to a superficially content but lifeless—and probably loveless—marriage. As he learns about this himself, Fr. Hugh tells his reader that "the edge of sadness was visible" in Helen.[39] "It was clear that she hadn't found . . . what? What we all hoped to find, I suppose."[40]

The second time the phrase occurs, Fr. Hugh is describing himself. Now that Fr. Hugh has been sober for more than five years, and seemingly has successfully learned to be an alcoholic, the bishop offers him a promotion of sorts to a wealthy, vibrant Irish parish, and away from the multiethnic but moribund parish to which he had been assigned after his return from the Cenacle. Having learned how to be an alcoholic, Father turns down the assignment, choosing to stay in his "lesser" parish. Returning to the shabby rectory, Fr. Hugh reflects on the decision he just made:

> This was the first time I'd ever stood, all alone, in the silence of this old building filled with little but the echoes of a past that was over before my own began, and looked around me, and slowly realized, at last, that this was mine and would be mine: that it was my home for the rest of my life. And with this at first I felt a touch of regret, *an edge of sadness*: I knew that as long as I lived in Old St. Paul's it would never mean to me what [prior prestigious assignments] had meant—that it could never grip my heart and affections the same way. And then, out of nowhere, a single question came before me: *Was it ever intended to*?[41]

The answer of course is no, it was not. Fr. Hugh had come to the realization that none of us are immune from the edge of sadness. It is a condition of fallen human nature. It is not clear whether Helen ever came to see this. But Fr. Hugh, in the dank, drafty, dilapidated rectory of Old St. Paul's came to realize that the edge of sadness may be the border of joy. Thus, "I might," he thought, "through the parish and its people, find my way not again to the simple engagement of the heart and affections, but to the Richness, the Mercy, the immeasurable Love of God."[42]

No one would recommend becoming an alcoholic in order to find a way to the richness, mercy, and immeasurable love of God. The vast majority of those who do find their way do so without going through the pain and humiliation of alcoholism. But through Fr. Hugh Kennedy, Edwin O'Connor tells us that God can work through many kinds of human imperfection. Sometimes he even uses those imperfections both as the means of salvation of the imperfect person and consolation for those the person is commissioned to help. Fr. Hugh crept up to the very edge of sadness. But from that edge, he was able to peer into joy. And the last day we hear from him, he has chosen to embrace the joy. One day at a time.

Acknowledgments

IT WAS NOT MY idea to write this book. And if I had not been prompted, I would never have contemplated writing such a book. But I am happy to have written it, and hopeful that it might help both alcoholics and the people who love them to understand how we alcoholics think and act. Thus, I am grateful to my friend Mike Aquilina for asking me to write it. Mike's request was not without some background. I have written short articles about my recovery on various occasions, beginning on the fifteenth anniversary of my sobriety in 2017. Mike read some of those pieces and suggested that I write a short book expanding on their themes and topics. I was reluctant at first because, as I had written in one of those articles, I don't think I have that much to say about it. But Mike encouraged me to think about it a bit more. I did. And the book you are holding is the fruit of that request and my rumination over it. Of course, the shortcomings in the book are all mine, but Mike's vision got the ball rolling.

I am grateful to Mike for his encouragement, and even more deeply to my wife, Sue Craycraft, for her unwavering support. Like so many spouses, parents, siblings, and children of alcoholics, Sue did not understand why I drank in excess. But she knew I did. And while she is not an expert in addiction, recovery, or human behavior, she is wise. She saw that my drinking was causing harm to our relationship, the security of our family, and my own health and safety. And she expressed that concern to me on multiple occasions. But she neither condemned nor excused me. And thus, she managed to walk that fine line between the Scylla of condemnation and the Charybdis of enablement.

In addition to being very wise, my wife is also the most prayerfully devoted Christian woman I know. Through my fifteen years or so of heavy drinking, she prayed without ceasing that I would moderate my drinking or, even better, stop altogether. Her prayers were as agonizingly tearful as they were doggedly persistent. Thus, on the one hand I am deeply remorseful for the pain and confusion that I caused her in those years. On the other hand, however, I am profoundly grateful for her unceasing intercession on my behalf. I gave Sue sufficient reason to give up on me, as I dismissed her concern or rebuffed her suggestions for cutting back. She loves me too much to do that. God's grace in answering my wife's prayers is the reason you have read this book rather than my premature obituary.

I love you, Sue. I owe my life to you. You are my St. Monica.

Additional Resources

Additional Novels on Addiction and Recovery

Graham Greene's novel *The Power and the Glory*[1] is an excellent account of the grip of alcohol addiction in the face of severe personal distress. The "Whiskey Priest" in *The Power and the Glory* resonates with many readers because of his halting but certain faith in the sacraments, even in the throes of addiction. Kirstin Valdez Quade has written an emotionally powerful and sympathetic story in her novel *The Five Wounds.*[2] It is the sympathetic story of one man's struggle against addiction and his own personal demons. And although it is less accessible than these or the novels discussed below, David Foster Wallace's *Infinite Jest*[3] is a majestic and penetrating analysis of the power of addiction. Wallace is not for the faint of heart, and *Infinite Jest* takes nearly infinite patience to read. But it is worth the effort. Jack London's *John Barleycorn,*[4] Thomas De Quincey's *Confessions of an English Opium Eater,*[5] and John Berryman's

Recovery[6] have stood the test of time as powerful stories about addiction.

Addiction and Recovery in Songs

Americana artists and recovering alcoholics Jason Isbell and Jason DeFord (performing as Jelly Roll) also illustrate the complexity of addiction and the difficulty of loving an addict.

In "Cover Me Up"[7] from Isbell's 2013 album *Southeastern*, Isbell exposes his own vulnerability as an addict and celebrates the perseverance of his wife in supporting him. The song accounts for what we might call the narrator's "rock bottom" experience, and the perseverance of the woman who loved him. But both the song and Isbell's life more broadly illustrate the necessity of a community to get and stay sober.

In "It Gets Easier"[8] from Isbell's 2020 album *Reunions*, the alcoholic narrator begins by recounting a dream that is familiar to every alcoholic: He dreamt that he had started drinking again. But the reason he knows it was merely a dream is that he had only one glass of wine and woke up without a hangover. That is something practicing alcoholics are certainly *not* familiar with! The addict knows that one glass of wine is both too many and not enough. But he also knows that the non-addict literally cannot understand this problem. As a non-alcoholic character in *The Lost Weekend* perceptively notes, "You and I don't realize it, because liquor doesn't mean to us what it means to them."[9]

Jelly Roll's song "Winning Streak,"[10] from his 2024 album *Beautifully Broken*, is a straight-up autobiographical song about DeFord's addiction and recovery. The song recounts his own first visit to an AA meeting, expressing both wonderment and gratitude that he was there. Both the lyrics and the song set the tone for this remarkable album of introspection and humble transparency. DeFord has been open about his struggle with alcohol and drug addiction, as well as his convictions in his youth for various crimes related to those addictions. And he has used his newfound fame as platform to advocate for addiction recovery programs, especially related to the opioid epidemic in the United States.

The entirety of the album *Beautifully Broken* is a sustained concrete meditation on the vices related to addiction and the virtues necessary for recovery. Along the way, DeFord explores the difficulty of admitting having an addiction, as well as the external forces that conspire to defeat his characters' struggle to recover. The first and fourth of the twelve steps of Alcoholics Anonymous are an admission that one is "powerless over alcohol," which makes one's life "unmanageable," and that the addict must make a "searching and fearless moral inventory" of himself. Although most of the other ten steps make appearances in the album, *Beautifully Broken* can be seen as an exposition of these two key steps.

DeFord writes with unflinching, raw honesty about the damage caused by addiction, but always balanced by a message of hope for recovery. Self-reflection and memory are necessary parts of this process. The addict cannot afford to try to escape his past. Rather, he must incorporate that past into the present—one step at a time—so that every day is a reminder of the power of addiction and the fragility of recovery. If we lose track of the mistakes and missteps that contributed to our addiction, we render ourselves vulnerable to making them again.

But most importantly, DeFord understands that his recovery is not possible without the grace of God, by which he has discovered the meaning and purpose that cannot be found at the bottom of a glass. That is the grace that tells us that we are both fallen and redeemable. For the addict, redemption is possible only to the extent that we remain vigilant about how painful it is to ourselves and others. As the brilliant singer-songwriter "Jelly Roll," Jason DeFord is an unlikely source of the grace that helps to keep me sober. But that's how God works. Grace is everywhere, even, sometimes, in the salty songs of a tattooed, hip-hop-and-country-singing drug addict.

Notes

Introduction

1. Martha Woodruff, "Sharing Demons with Hank Williams," *The New York Times Magazine*, August 13, 2010, https://www.nytimes.com/2010/08/15/magazine/15lives-t.html.

2. Augustine of Hippo, *Confessions*, trans. Thomas Williams (Hackett, 2019), 8.18, p. 151.

3. Augustine, *Confessions*, 8.18, p. 152.

4. See the appendix for my recommendations for additional novels.

5. Charles Jackson, *The Lost Weekend* (Random House, 1944; repr., Vintage Books Edition, 2013).

6. Malcolm Lowry, *Under the Volcano* (Reynal & Hitchcock, 1947; repr., Penguin, 2005).

7. Evelyn Waugh, *Brideshead Revisited* (Little, Brown, 1945; repr., Word on Fire, 2024).

8. Edwin O'Connor, *The Edge of Sadness* (Little, Brown, 1962; repr., Loyola Classics, 2005).

Chapter 1: Narrativity and Virtue

1. Stanley Hauerwas, *The Peaceable Kingdom: A Primer in Christian Ethics* (University of Notre Dame Press, 1983), p. 33.

2. Alasdair MacIntyre, *After Virtue: A Study in Moral Theory*, 2nd ed. (University of Notre Dame Press, 1984), p. 144.

3. When I use the phrase *moral action*, I mean an action that has moral content, open to moral judgment, not necessarily a "good" action. A "bad" action is a "bad moral action."

4. MacIntyre, *After Virtue*, p. 144.

5. Robert Barron, *The Great Story of Israel* (Word on Fire, 2024), p. 71.

6. *Shema* is a transliteration of the imperative form of the verb "hear."

7. Hauerwas, *Peaceable Kingdom*, p. 24.

8. Hauerwas, *Peaceable Kingdom*, pp. 24–25.

9. Hauerwas, *Peaceable Kingdom*, p. 26.

10. Hauerwas, *Peaceable Kingdom*, p. 26.

11. Hauerwas, *Peaceable Kingdom*, p. 25.

12. Representative examples of postmodern theorists include Jacque Derrida, Jean-François Lyotard, and Michel Foucault.

13. Hauerwas, *Peaceable Kingdom*, p. 29.

14. Hauerwas, *Peaceable Kingdom*, p. 29.

15. Hauerwas, *Peaceable Kingdom*, p. 33.

16. Hauerwas, *Peaceable Kingdom*, p. 34. For a fuller account of the narrative character of Christian moral theology, see Stanley Hauerwas and David Burrell, CSC, "From System to Story: An Alternative Pattern for Rationality in Ethics," in Stanley Hauerwas and L. Gregory Jones, ed., *Why Narrative? Readings in Narrative Theology* (Eerdmans, 1989), pp. 158–190.

17. Hauerwas and Burrell, "From System to Story," p. 190.

18. Aristotle, *Nicomachean Ethics*, trans. Terence Irwin (Hackett, 1999), 1094a 1–2. Rather than refer to page numbers in this translation, I utilize the uniform pagination of Aristotle's works known as "Bekker" numbers, named for August Bekker, the nineteenth-century German scholar who invented the universal way of citing Aristotle. This way, one can find the reference regardless of the translation or edition of Aristotle's works.

19. Aristotle, *Nicomachean Ethics*, 1094a 7–10.

20. Aristotle, *Nicomachean Ethics*, 1094a 11–12.

21. Aristotle, *Nicomachean Ethics*, 1098a 8–10.

22. Aristotle, *Nicomachean Ethics*, 1098a 12–13.

23. Aristotle, *Nicomachean Ethics*, 1098a 13–15.

24. *Catechism of the Catholic Church*, 2nd ed. (Libreria Editrice Vaticana–United States Conference of Catholic Bishops, 2000), no. 1803. Hereon cited as *CCC*.

25. *CCC*, no. 1804.

26. *CCC*, no. 1803, quoting Gregory of Nyssa, *De beatitudinibus*, 1: PG 44, 1200D.

27. *CCC*, no. 1804.

28. My purpose in this book is not to give a complete account of virtue and the virtues. For an account of the cardinal virtues, see Josef Pieper, *The Four Cardinal Virtues*, trans. Richard Winston (University of Notre Dame Press, 1966).

29. Romanus Cessario, OP, *Introduction to Moral Theology* (The Catholic University of America Press, 2001), p. 128.

30. Cessario, *Introduction to Moral Theology*, p. 136.

31. Cessario, *Introduction to Moral Theology*, p. 148, n. 69.

32. Cessario, *Introduction to Moral Theology*, p. 136.

33. *CCC*, no. 1809.

34. Pieper, *The Four Cardinal Virtues*, p. 147.

35. Pieper goes on to explain that "there are two modes of turning toward the self: a selfless and a selfish one. Only the former makes for self-preservation; the latter is destructive." Pieper, *The Four Cardinal Virtues*, pp. 147–148.

36. Pieper, *The Four Cardinal Virtues*, p. 148.

Chapter 2: *The Lost Weekend*: One Is Too Many and a Hundred Not Enough

1. Jackson, *Lost Weekend*, p. 39.

2. I must issue one qualification here, which I explore more fully in chapters 3 and 4 in my discussions of Geoffrey Firmin (*Under the Volcano*) and Sebastian Flyte (*Brideshead Revisited*). Although I have had a happy adulthood, I had a very unhappy childhood. Indeed, some might describe it as tragic. Whether, or to the extent, that it contributed to my later alcoholism is a question I explore below in the context of the lives of these two characters. For now, I merely note that I will neither blame nor discount my childhood trauma as a contributing cause to my drinking. And even in this later discussion, as you will see, I do not land on a definitive answer, but only explore possibilities.

3. Differential diagnosis is the clinical process of eliminating possible causes of certain symptoms in order to arrive at the most probable cause of them. It is the process of determining what is *not* the disease or condition to arrive at a *likely* diagnosis from the remaining possibilities. Differential diagnosis does not land on a definitive cause but tries to isolate the most likely illness or condition causing the presenting symptoms. This allows the health care worker and patient to determine the

most hopeful course of treatment or care, while not closing off the possibility of more definitive information in the course of treatment.

4. In 1945, *The Lost Weekend* was adapted into a highly successful film of the same name, screenplay written by Billy Wilder and Charles Brackett, produced by Brackett and directed by Wilder. The film won four Academy Awards: best picture (Brackett), best director (Wilder), best actor (Ray Milland), and best adapted screenplay (Wilder and Brackett). Jackson cooperated with the production of the film version but was dissatisfied with the ending, which is significantly different from the ending of the novel. My treatment in this chapter is solely related to the novel, although I do discuss below the two different endings in order to further my own argument about Don Birnham's alcoholism and addiction more generally. For a discussion of the development of the screenplay, see Blake Bailey's excellent book, *Farther & Wilder: The Lost Weekends and Literary Dreams of Charles Jackson* (Knopf, 2013), pp. 181–205.

5. Leslie Jamison, *The Recovering: Intoxication and its Aftermath* (Little, Brown, 2018), p. 74.

6. For biographical details about Charles Jackson's own alcohol and drug addictions, including his several relapses, hospitalizations, and suicide, see generally Bailey, *Farther & Wilder*, especially p. 250 and p. 305.

7. Jackson, *Lost Weekend*, p. 21.

8. Jackson, *Lost Weekend*, p. 4 (emphasis in original).

9. Jackson, *Lost Weekend*, p. 5.

10. Jackson, *Lost Weekend*, p. 5.

11. Tolstoy's sentence is, "Happy families are all alike; every unhappy family is unhappy in its own way." Leo Tolstoy, *Anna*

Karenina, trans. Constance Garnett (Planet, 2012), Kindle edition, p. 8.

12. "Remember that we deal with alcohol—cunning, baffling, and powerful!" *Alcoholics Anonymous: The Story of How Many Thousands of Men and Women Have Recovered from Alcoholism*, 4th ed. (Alcoholics Anonymous World Service, 2001), p. 31.

13. Jackson, *Lost Weekend*, p. 41.

14. Jackson, *Lost Weekend*, p. 41.

15. Jackson, *Lost Weekend*, p. 224.

16. Jackson, *Lost Weekend*, p. 224.

17. Cessario, *Introduction to Moral Theology*, p. 93.

18. Cessario, *Introduction to Moral Theology*, p. 93.

19. Jackson, *Lost Weekend*, p. 145.

20. Jackson, *Lost Weekend*, p. 144.

21. Jackson, *Lost Weekend*, p. 181.

22. Jackson, *Lost Weekend*, p. 181.

23. Jackson, *Lost Weekend*, p. 181.

24. Jackson, *Lost Weekend*, p. 181.

25. Jackson, *Lost Weekend*, p. 224.

26. Jackson, *Lost Weekend*, p. 224.

27. Quoted in Bailey, *Farther & Wilder*, p. 182.

28. Quoted in Bailey, *Farther & Wilder*, p. 183.

Chapter 3: *Under the Volcano*: There's No Bargaining with Alcohol

1. Of course, the same does not hold for pharmacological solutions to many other chronic diseases or conditions related to normal nutrition, hydration, or exercise. Treatment for digestive

issues or genetic intolerance of some foods is a good thing. Nor, of course, does my analysis apply to medical technologies for overcoming physical or even cognitive disabilities.

2. Lowry, *Under the Volcano*, p. 50.

3. Jamison, *The Recovering*, p. 73.

4. Jamison, *The Recovering*, pp. 73–74. Jamison generally cites John Crowley, *The White Logic: Alcoholism and Gender in America* (University of Massachusetts, 1994).

5. Don "didn't drink because he liked the taste (actually whisky was dreadful to the palate; he swallowed at once to get it down as quickly as possible): he drank for what it did to him." Jackson, p. 41.

6. Lowry, *Under the Volcano*, p. 48.

7. Lowry, *Under the Volcano*, p. 38.

8. Lowry, *Under the Volcano*, p. 19.

9. Alcoholics Anonymous, p. 31.

10. Stanley Hauerwas, *Hannah's Child: A Theologian's Memoir* (Eerdmans, 2010), p. 242. This discussion of self-deception is adapted from Kenneth Craycraft, "Say My Name: Self-Deception, Transparency, and Redemption in the Breaking Bad Universe," *Church Life Journal*, July 5, 2023, https://churchlifejournal.nd.edu.

11. David Burrell and Stanley Hauerwas, "Self-Deception and Autobiography: Theological and Ethical Reflections on Speer's *Inside the Third Reich*," in Hauerwas, *Truthfulness and Tragedy: Further Investigations into Christian Ethics* (University of Notre Dame Press, 1977), p. 82.

12. Burrell and Hauerwas, "Self-Deception and Autobiography," p. 84.

13. Burrell and Hauerwas, "Self-Deception and Autobiography," p. 86.

14. Burrell and Hauerwas, "Self-Deception and Autobiography," p. 86.

15. Burrell and Hauerwas, "Self-Deception and Autobiography," p. 86.

16. Lowry, *Under the Volcano*, p. 223.

17. "Not a bullfight?" asks Yvonne. "No, a bullthrowing," responds the Consul. Lowry, *Under the Volcano*, p. 189.

18. Lowry, *Under the Volcano*, pp. 148–149.

19. Lowry, *Under the Volcano*, p. 149.

20. Lowry, *Under the Volcano*, p. 109. Geoffrey claimed to be working on a book of comparative spirituality, but it was probably just a fantasy. "Geoffrey said something this morning about going on with his book—for the life of me I don't know whether he's still writing one or not, he's never done any work on it since I've known him, and he's never let me see scarcely any of it." *Under the Volcano*, p. 150.

21. Lowry, *Under the Volcano*, p. 48.

22. Lowry, *Under the Volcano*, p. 48.

23. Lowry, *Under the Volcano*, p. 48.

24. Lowry, *Under the Volcano*, p. 61.

25. Lowry, *Under the Volcano*, p. 161.

26. Martha Woodroof, "Sharing Demons with Hank Williams," *The New York Times Magazine*, August 13, 2010, p. 50.

Chapter 4: *Brideshead Revisited*: It's the *Way* an Alcoholic Drinks

1. The other six signs of Jesus's divinity in the Gospel of John are: 2. Healing of the official's son (4:46–54); 3. Healing of the

paralytic at Bethesda (5:1–18); 4. Feeding the five thousand (6:5–15); 5. Walking on water (6:16–21); 6. Healing the man born blind (9:1–41); and 7. Raising Lazarus from the dead (11:1–44).

2. Waugh, *Brideshead Revisited*.

3. Evelyn Waugh, *Helena* (Chapman & Hall, 1950).

4. Evelyn Waugh, *Men at Arms* (Chapman & Hall, 1952); *Officers and Gentlemen* (Chapman & Hall, 1955); *Unconditional Surrender* (Chapman & Hall, 1961).

5. Anthony Andrews won both BAFTA and Golden Globe television awards for his performance. Coincidentally, Andrews also played Hugh Firmin in the 1984 film adaptation of *Under the Volcano*. And for audiobook listeners, Jeremy Irons narrates the Hachette Audio edition of *Brideshead Revisited* (2012).

6. Waugh, *Brideshead Revisited*, p. 111.

7. Waugh, *Brideshead Revisited*, p. 23.

8. Waugh, *Brideshead Revisited*, p. 23.

9. Waugh, *Brideshead Revisited*, pp. 23–24.

10. Waugh, *Brideshead Revisited*, p. 23.

11. Waugh, *Brideshead Revisited*, p. 24. When Charles explains that it was not someone from his party but rather someone from outside the college, Lunt answers, "Well, it's just as nasty clearing it up, whoever it was." Waugh, *Brideshead Revisited*, p. 24.

12. Waugh, *Brideshead Revisited*, p. 36.

13. Waugh, *Brideshead Revisited*, p. 30.

14. Waugh, *Brideshead Revisited*, p. 32.

15. Waugh, *Brideshead Revisited*, p. 32.

16. Before Charles had met Sebastian, he knew about him through Sebastian's flamboyant exploits, including his prominent teddy bear. "My first sight of him was in the door of Germer's," Charles explains, "and, on that occasion, I was struck less by his

looks than by the fact that he was carrying a large teddy-bear." Noticing Charles's censorious glare as Sebastian left the shop, the barber asks Charles, "What do you suppose Lord Sebastian wanted? A hair brush for his teddy-bear; it had to have very stiff bristles, *not*, Lord Sebastian said, to brush him with, but to threaten him with a spanking when he was sulky. He bought a very nice one with an ivory back, and he's having 'Aloysius' engraved on it." Waugh, *Brideshead Revisited*, pp. 22–23. Inviting Charles to lunch the day after Sebastian vomits into Charles's room, Sebastian says, "Aloysius won't speak to me until he sees I am forgiven." Waugh, *Brideshead Revisited*, p. 24. In a letter to Charles saying that he is going to visit his father in Venice, Sebastian writes, "I have a good mind not to take Aloysius to Venice. I don't want him to meet a lot of horrid Italian bears and pick up bad habits." Waugh, *Brideshead Revisited*, p. 62.

17. Although, of course, *Brideshead Revisited* is fiction, Sebastian's similarity to the respective childhoods of Don Birnam and Geoffrey Firmin cannot be ignored. The insecurity caused by the absent father, regardless of the reason for the absence, is a thread that runs through these novels. As we will see in chapter 5, a variation on the theme is also found in Edwin O'Connor's *The Edge of Sadness.*

18. Waugh, *Brideshead Revisited*, pp. 72–73.

19. Waugh, *Brideshead Revisited*, p. 89.

20. Waugh, *Brideshead Revisited*, pp. 88–89.

21. Waugh, *Brideshead Revisited*, p. 90.

22. Waugh, *Brideshead Revisited*, p. 90.

23. Waugh, *Brideshead Revisited*, p. 90.

24. Waugh, *Brideshead Revisited*, p. 106.

25. Waugh, *Brideshead Revisited*, p. 107.

26. Waugh, *Brideshead Revisited*, p. 109.
27. Waugh, *Brideshead Revisited*, p. 111.
28. Waugh, *Brideshead Revisited*, p. 114.
29. Waugh, *Brideshead Revisited*, p. 115.
30. Waugh, *Brideshead Revisited*, p. 119.
31. Waugh, *Brideshead Revisited*, p. 121.
32. Waugh, *Brideshead Revisited*, p. 122.
33. Waugh, *Brideshead Revisited*, p. 114.
34. Waugh, *Brideshead Revisited*, p. 130.
35. Waugh, *Brideshead Revisited*, p. 284.
36. Waugh, *Brideshead Revisited*, p. 284.
37. Graham Greene, *Brighton Rock* (Penguin, 1938), p. 246.

Chapter 5: *The Edge of Sadness*: On Learning to Be an Alcoholic

1. This requires a significant caveat. Since our children have grown, married, and had children of their own, our house is a busier destination of gatherings than ever before. But the kinds of dinner parties for friends and associates that we used to host are far less frequent. This would be the case anyway, because grandkids have priority!

2. After being out of print for many years, a fine edition of *The Edge of Sadness* was republished by Cluny Media in 2025. All references in this book, however, are to the Loyola Classics edition.

3. Whether Evelyn Waugh was an alcoholic is an open question. He was a very heavy drinker, especially toward the end of his life. And it is probable that the mode and amount of Waugh's drinking met the criteria for alcoholism. But he never expressly

considered himself an alcoholic, nor was he ever treated as one. His late novel, *The Ordeal of Gilbert Pinfold* (Little Brown, 1957), is a deliberate fictionalized account of an episode in which Waugh confessed that "Three years ago I had quite a new experience. I went off my head for about three weeks." See Douglas Lane Patey, *The Life of Evelyn Waugh* (Blackwell, 1998), p. 339. By all accounts, this was an acute episode brought on by a combination of financial worries, alcohol, and a sleeping draught that Waugh frequently imbibed.

4. O'Connor died suddenly from a stroke on March 23, 1968, a few of months before his fiftieth birthday. See "Edwin O'Connor Dies of Stroke; Author of 'The Last Hurrah,' 49," *The New York Times*, March 24, 1968, p. 92.

5. O'Connor, *Edge of Sadness*, p. 57.

6. O'Connor, *Edge of Sadness*, p. 57.

7. O'Connor, *Edge of Sadness*, p. 75.

8. O'Connor, *Edge of Sadness*, p. 75.

9. O'Connor, *Edge of Sadness*, p. 75.

10. O'Connor, *Edge of Sadness*, p. 76.

11. O'Connor, *Edge of Sadness*, p. 76.

12. O'Connor, *Edge of Sadness*, p. 77.

13. O'Connor, *Edge of Sadness*, p. 77.

14. A caveat: As explained below, Fr. Hugh had been sober for more than four years when this dinner party occurred. But much of that time had been spent far away from New England, at a treatment center in Arizona. His sobriety was thus "new" to those who had not seen him for several years, including Agnes. See the discussion to follow.

15. O'Connor, *Edge of Sadness*, p. 9.

16. See John Kenneth Galbraith, "Sadness in Boston," in *The New Yorker*, no. 19, June 24, 1961, pp. 87–94.

17. If you have read *Brideshead Revisited*, you know that it is not completely accurate to say that Lord Alexander Marchmain did not return to the family. But his "return" was not a reconciliation; and besides that, Sebastian had long since disappeared in North Africa when Lord Marchmain returned to England toward the end of the novel.

18. O'Connor, *Edge of Sadness*, p. 181–182.

19. O'Connor, *Edge of Sadness*, p. 182.

20. O'Connor, *Edge of Sadness*, p. 176,

21. O'Connor, *Edge of Sadness*, p. 184.

22. O'Connor, *Edge of Sadness*, p. 185.

23. O'Connor, *Edge of Sadness*, p. 185.

24. O'Connor, *Edge of Sadness*, p. 186.

25. O'Connor, *Edge of Sadness*, p. 186.

26. O'Connor, *Edge of Sadness*, p. 186.

27. O'Connor, *Edge of Sadness*, p. 186–187.

28. O'Connor, *Edge of Sadness*, p. 187.

29. O'Connor, *Edge of Sadness*, pp. 188–189.

30. O'Connor, *Edge of Sadness*, p. 191.

31. O'Connor, *Edge of Sadness*, p. 192.

32. O'Connor, *Edge of Sadness*, p. 192.

33. O'Connor, *Edge of Sadness*, pp. 198–199.

34. O'Connor, *Edge of Sadness*, p. 201.

35. O'Connor, *Edge of Sadness*, pp. 204–205.

36. O'Connor, *Edge of Sadness*, p. 206.

37. O'Connor, *Edge of Sadness*, p. 208.

38. O'Connor, *Edge of Sadness*, p. 209.

39. O'Connor, *Edge of Sadness*, p. 566.
40. O'Connor, *Edge of Sadness*, p. 566.
41. O'Connor, *Edge of Sadness*, pp. 636–637.
42. O'Connor, *Edge of Sadness*, p. 637.

Additional Resources

1. Graham Greene, *The Power and the Glory* (Penguin, 2015).
2. Kirstin Valdez Quade, *The Five Wounds* (Norton, 2021).
3. David Foster Wallace, *Infinite Jest* (Little, Brown, 1996).
4. Jack London, *John Barleycorn* (Aegitas, 2016).
5. Thomas De Quincey, *Confessions of an English Opium Eater* (Penguin, 2003).
6. John Berryman, *Recovery* (University of Minnesota Press, 2016).
7. "Cover Me Up," track 1 on Jason Isbell, *Southeastern*, Southeastern Records, 2013.
8. "It Gets Easier," track 9 on Jason Isbell, *Reunions*, Southeastern Records, 2020.
9. Jackson, *Lost Weekend*, p. 137.
10. "Winning Streak," track 1 on Jelly Roll, *Beautifully Broken*, Bailee & Buddy, 2024.